THE
LIVING
TRUST
HANDBOOK

**This complete and practical guide
will show you how to:**

- Avoid probate and conservatorship

- Reduce or eliminate estate and death income taxes

- Maintain privacy

BY ATTORNEY
David E. Miller

Printed and published in the United States
by David E. Miller Law Corporation
601 Van Ness Avenue
Suite 2050
San Francisco, CA 94102
(415) 776-5100

THE DAVID E. MILLER LAW CORPORATION
also has branch offices in San Jose,
Pleasant Hill and San Mateo, CA.

This book has been written to explain to you the many positive advantages of establishing a Complete Estate Plan using the Living Trust as the primary vehicle to save money for you and your loved ones and to give you peace of mind about the future.

David E. Miller is an attorney who specializes exclusively in estate planning. A practicing attorney for over 25 years, he graduated from Ohio State College of Law in 1964 with a Doctor of Jurisprudence degree. He is a member of the California, Ohio, Washington, D.C., New York and Virginia state bars. He is also admitted to practice before the United States Supreme Court, the United States Tax Court and the United States Court of Appeals. His previous experience includes being an Assistant Attorney General for the State of Ohio and a Lieutenant Commander in the United States Navy. He has been a frequent guest on both KGO and KCBS radio to discuss the Living Trust. He has lived in the San Francisco Bay Area for over 20 years. He is married and has three children, ages 11, 13 and 15.

All statements made in this book are based upon California and federal laws, rules and regulations in effect in 1991 (we know they're a mess, but they're what we have to work with). This book necessarily has to deal with general principles and should not be considered legal advice concerning your specific situation.

Contents

Chapter

Appendix

Chapter 1
Why Do I Need an Estate Plan?

"Nothing is certain except death and taxes." Nothing in this book can help with the first certainty, but it can help with the taxes and the other costs involved when we all meet our eventual fate.

We all have an estate plan, it's just that most of us don't know what it is. The sad fact is that if you don't plan your estate, the government will do it for you. It will decide who your heirs are, what they will get, when they will get it and how much to charge them for taxes and probate costs. All this without consulting you.

But you <u>can</u> take control of the situation. The simple answer to the question as to why you should plan your estate is to save money and to obtain peace of mind.

We have no doubt that if you take the time to read this book, you will be convinced that taking an active part in your own estate planning makes sense. But be careful — a bad estate plan may be worse than no estate plan at all.

"We have too many lawyers." "We have too many laws." "Our laws are too complex." The author of this book is a lawyer, but he agrees with these sentiments. But don't put your head in the sand. Take advantage of the laws, don't let them take advantage of you. Your objective should be to plan now so you and your family can have as little future need for, and involvement with, lawyers, courts, executors, administrators, conservators, the IRS and other such types.

We recommend what we call a "Complete Estate Plan" which will do the following for you and your family:

- Allow you to choose your heirs and decide when they will receive their inheritance.
- Avoid probate.
- Eliminate or reduce federal estate taxes.

Chapter 1

Why Do I Need an Estate Plan?

- Eliminate death income taxes.
- Avoid conservatorship.
- Maintain control over your assets.
- Maintain flexibility.
- Maintain privacy.
- Provide for health care and other decisions if you become incapacitated.
- Provide for funeral and burial instructions.
- Provide for anatomical gifts (if you so desire).
- Make the administration of your estate as quick, inexpensive and easy as possible.

Remember, either you can do this for yourself and your family or you can let the government do it for you. The government's record in looking out for your interests has not been good. We think you can do better for yourself.

We believe that for most people a Complete Estate Plan centered around a Living Trust makes the most sense because it does the best job of accomplishing all of your objectives.

In this chapter we would like to explain why you want to avoid probate, why you want to avoid conservatorship, how federal estate taxes work and how they can be reduced or eliminated and how death income taxes work and how they can be eliminated. Chapters 2 through 5 will discuss the most common

forms of estate plans and will show you why they will fail to meet many, if not all, of your objectives. Chapter 6 will discuss the Living Trust and show you why it makes the most sense for most of you as the centerpiece of a Complete Estate Plan. Chapter 7 will discuss what you need to do in addition to establishing a Living Trust to have a Complete Estate Plan. Chapter 8 will tell you what you can do right now to begin and complete your Complete Estate Plan. Chapter 9 will explain how your Complete Estate Plan could work for you during your lifetime, and for your family after your death and after your spouse's death. Chapter 10 contains a summary of some of the most important points in the book in question and answer form and also a lot of new information (just to make sure you'll finish the book).

Avoidance of Probate

What is probate and why should it be avoided? What is hell and why should it be avoided?

The answer to the first question is a little less obvious than to the second, but if you'll ask someone who's gone through the probate process, the two questions are not that dissimilar.

The avoidance of probate is the single most important reason to use a Living Trust as the centerpiece of your Com-

Why Do I Need an Estate Plan?

plete Estate Plan.

What is probate? Simply put, it is the process by which your estate is gathered together, title to your property established, adverse claims to your property determined, liabilities and taxes paid and the remainder distributed to your heirs. Sounds simple? Read on.

Why should probate be avoided? Simply put, to avoid loss of time, loss of money, loss of privacy and loss of peace of mind.

Following is a short summary of the steps involved in the probate process:

- Petition the court for probate of the will (Time).
- Obtain a court order for the appointment of an executor (Time).
- Post bond if not waived or executor is not the sole beneficiary (Money).
- Give notice to creditors of the probate estate (Time).
- Petition the court for widow's or family allowance (Time).
- Assemble, conserve and inventory the assets (Time).
- Appraise the assets (Time and Money).
- Obtain court orders to deal with assets (Time and Money).
- Settle all proper claims (Time).
- Deal with the problems of any going business (Time and Money).
- Obtain bids in court before the sale of real estate (Time and Money).
- Obtain court approval for sales of stock (Time and Money).
- Obtain court approval for any necessary borrowing (Time and Money).
- Obtain a court order to distribute the estate (Time).
- Pay executor's and attorney's fees (Money).

How much time and how much money does probate involve? You can generally count on nine months to one year to complete your probate — if you're lucky. It could take longer. Two years is not uncommon where there are "problems" with your estate. We know that none of you are counting on any problems with your estate. That only happens to other people, right?

What are the basic costs of probate? (Remember, these are probate costs only, not income or estate taxes, which will be discussed separately.) The California Probate Code sets out certain basic statutory fees for executors and attorneys. In effect, these are <u>minimum</u> fees. If any work is done beyond the minimum expected, the executor or the attorney or both may petition the court for additional fees. These are called "extraordinary" fees, but, unfortunately, "extraordinary" fees are awarded for some pretty ordinary services. Extraor-

Chapter 1

Why Do I Need an Estate Plan?

Probate of a Simple Estate

- Person named in will as executor obtains original will and any codicils.

- Person named in will as executor selects an attorney (usually, but not always, the attorney who prepared the will).

- Attorney files petition with the Probate Court to probate will and officially name the person selected in the will to be the executor of the estate.

- Attorney, on behalf of the person named in the will as executor, publishes notice of death and mails notice to heirs.

- Court admits will to probate and appoints an executor.

- Executor collects assets and files inventory.

- Executor sells estate assets.

- Executor pays debts.

- Executor's accountant prepares and files estate tax and income tax returns.

- Executor pays estate taxes and income taxes.

- Executor prepares an accounting and files a petition with the Probate Court to conclude the estate.

- Executor pays statutory and extraordinary executor's and attorney's fees.

- Executor delivers remaining assets to heirs.

Why Do I Need an Estate Plan?

dinary fees are often awarded for filing state and federal income tax and estate tax returns, selling estate assets, conducting the decedent's business or defending the estate against claims filed in the probate court. Sort of makes you wonder what the minimum fee was for, doesn't it?

In reviewing the fee chart below, you must be aware that statutory probate fees are based on your gross estate, not your net estate. For example, if you own a $200,000 home with a $150,000 mortgage, you have real estate that's worth $50,000 to you. But you will be charged probate fees based on the $200,000 gross value, not on the $50,000 net value. As you can see from the chart below, minimum probate fees would be more than $10,000 on this home.

Gross Probate Estate	Statutory Fees
$ 75,000	4,800
100,000	6,300
150,000	8,300
200,000	10,300
300,000	14,300
400,000	18,300
500,000	22,300
1,000,000	42,300

Take a look at Appendix C in the back of this book for the exact way to compute statutory probate fees and a more complete chart of examples.

With our inflated residential real estate prices, most of us who own a home have some very real concerns about probate costs. Stated another way, if you own a home, you probably need a Living Trust.

You can escape the time, expense and publicity of probate if your gross estate is small enough. Generally speaking, if your gross estate is worth less than $60,000, you don't have to go through the probate process. Take a look at Appendix B at the back of this book for the affidavit you use to transfer assets when your gross estate is worth less than $60,000. If you paid for this book (which we hope you did) and your gross estate is less than $60,000, you might want to try to sell the book to one of your wealthier friends. Actually, finishing the book wouldn't be such a bad idea. At seven percent inflation, the value of your estate will double every ten years. A $40,000 estate may well be worth $80,000 in ten years and $160,000 in twenty years. The combination of inflation, taxes and probate fees is the greatest enemy you have in your effort to accumulate and maintain wealth.

You might well ask yourself at this point, who would know or care if I didn't go through the probate process? Why

Chapter 1

Why Do I Need an Estate Plan?

Assets That Avoid Probate

- Assets transferred to a Living Trust.

- Insurance benefits (unless your estate is named as beneficiary).

- Retirement plan benefits, such as IRAs, pension plans, etc. (unless your estate is named as beneficiary).

- Assets held in joint tenancy.

- Totten trust bank accounts.

- All other assets if their total gross value is less than $60,000.

Why Do I Need an Estate Plan?

not just leave things in the name of my deceased spouse or parent? That might work for a while with a simple estate, but the moment you try to sell something, you're going to have to go through the probate process to put the property in your name before you can sell it. By then, you may well be delinquent in paying estate taxes, and you know your Uncle Sam doesn't appreciate delinquent tax returns. Your Uncle will be talking to you about penalties and interest.

Several years ago the American Bar Association recommended that each state adopt a new Model Probate Code which was designed to simplify the probate process and decrease probate costs. Unfortunately, not much progress has been made. There is a vested interest in the legal community in keeping things the way they are. As you can see, legal fees to probate an estate are generous. Legal fees to set up a Complete Estate Plan using a Living Trust will be relatively modest if you select an attorney experienced in the field (more on this later). There's no real incentive for the legal profession to modify the Probate Code any more than there is to recommend the Living Trust, which can completely eliminate the need for probate.

More bad news — if you own real estate in states other than the state in which you or your spouse dies, separate probate procedures have to be set up in each state, following that state's laws and involving that state's attorneys, probate courts and fee schedules. These are called ancillary probate procedures. More time and more money.

Remember, if you're a married person, you've got two sets of probate fees to worry about before your estate gets to your heirs. Let's assume the husband dies first (men, we know that's the way it's likely to be, whether we like it or not). Probate fees are based on his half of the gross value of the community property and the full value of his separate property, if any. Assuming he leaves everything to his wife, she is now the sole owner of 100% of the gross estate, and when she passes away probate fees are assessed <u>again</u> on the full value of the gross estate. The half of the husband's estate that has already been subjected to probate fees gets hit again. Two large bites have been taken out of the apple before anything gets to the children. And that doesn't count estate taxes, which we'll discuss later.

But, even if probate was free, you would still want to avoid it. One of the greatest dangers of the probate process is that because it's slow and cumbersome, the value of your assets will decline before they can be distributed. Just think of the times you've heard the term "pro-

Chapter 1

Why Do I Need an Estate Plan?

bate sale" or "estate sale" and associated it with "bargain sale." While a probate sale is often a buyer's bonanza, it's also often sadly a forced liquidation by the estate to pay taxes and probate costs. The bargain hunters will be there and they will find their bargains at the expense of you and your family unless you take control of the situation by planning your estate to avoid probate and minimize taxes.

If you happen to own a business you can only just begin to understand the chaos that would be caused by the death of you or your spouse and then the added imposition and expense of the probate process at just the wrong moment. Many small businesses, built up with a lifetime of work, have failed to survive the probate process.

In addition to losing time, money and peace of mind through the probate process, you also lose privacy. Everything about your estate — your assets, your liabilities, creditors' claims against you, taxes — all become part of the public record. Anyone can review and copy your probate file just by going to the courthouse. In an era where privacy is becoming harder and harder to maintain, this is the final blow. One of the most important features of the Living Trust is that <u>only</u> <u>you</u> <u>and</u> <u>those</u> <u>you</u> <u>choose</u> need know anything about your estate.

You might think, well I'll be gone, so it really doesn't make much difference. Of course you might just think that about <u>every</u> aspect of estate planning, not just loss of privacy. But remember, if you're married, <u>you</u> might be the surviving spouse and <u>you</u> would be left with the loss of time, money, peace of mind and privacy involved with probate and <u>you</u> will have to deal with estate and income taxes and lawyers and executors and the probate court and the IRS, etc., etc.

We know that this makes you sound selfish, but what we're really trying to show you is that you're <u>unintentionally</u> being selfish by not planning your estate. Statistics show that 70% of you don't have a will and that <u>99%</u> of you don't have a Living Trust. We believe that a Complete Estate Plan is one of the greatest gifts you can give your family — and yourself.

Before leaving the topic, you might well ask if there's any advantage at all of going through the probate process. Actually, there is one. If your estate is probated all those with claims against your estate must present those claims within four months after notice of death is published by your executor and assets distributed. In effect, the probate process creates a new four month statute of limitations that overrides all other statutes of limitations. If there's anything

Why Do I Need an Estate Plan?

Advantages and Disadvantages of Probate

Advantages

- Short statute of limitations to cut off creditor claims.

Disadvantages

- Loss of money.

- Loss of time.

- Loss of privacy.

- Loss of control.

- Loss of peace of mind.

Chapter 1

Why Do I Need an Estate Plan?

that rivals the probate process for sheer agony, it's the civil litigation system, with cases dragging out two to five or more years. If you're a person who's likely to be involved with protracted litigation, like an uninsured doctor with possible malpractice claims, you might just want to consider probating a portion of your assets to attempt to cut off creditor claims.

For example, Bing Crosby was one of the more famous users of the Living Trust. He was an extremely wealthy man, who was involved in a number of complex business transactions and also was aware that in our litigious society that he might be involved with one or more lawsuits in the future. Virtually all of his assets went to his heirs in complete privacy through his Living Trust, but he did choose to probate a small portion of his estate to cut off creditor claims.

Most of us don't have to worry about this, but for those of us that do, it is part of the planning that needs to be done in order to have a Complete Estate Plan.

Remember, the best way to deal with estate problems is to deal with them in advance.

Avoiding Estate Taxes

We're going to put aside the problems of probate now and deal with the second vital area of concern in proper estate planning — minimizing the amount we have to pay the government for the privilege of passing our assets on to our heirs.

Until recently this section of the book would have had to be divided into two parts, federal and state death taxes. Fortunately, in 1982 David Miller, the author of this book, sponsored a California initiative in which the voters bypassed the legislature and eliminated the need for any of us to be concerned about California inheritance taxes. Many other states have followed the California model, but if you live outside of California you should check on your own state laws.

Actually there still is a California estate tax. The federal law allows a credit for a certain amount of state estate tax paid. The California tax, if applicable at all, is the maximum allowed to take advantage of the federal credit. If you pay any estate tax at all, you pay the same amount you would if there were no California tax, but this way part of your money goes to Sacramento instead of to Washington, D.C. That way it gets to be wasted locally instead of nationally.

The purpose of this section is to give you an overview of the federal estate tax and to show you how to properly plan your estate to eliminate, or at least minimize, the effects of the estate tax.

Why Do I Need an Estate Plan?

We're not going to try to make you into estate tax attorneys, but we are going to show you a way many of you will not ever have to deal with estate tax attorneys if you do your planning now.

The first thing you need to know is that the estate tax, unlike probate fees, is computed on your net estate, not your gross estate. In order to decide on the best estate plan for yourself, you need to make an estimate of your net worth. List your assets — all your assets — and then decide the current fair market value of each one. Add together all the values and then add in the death benefit of your life insurance. We know many of you believe that life insurance proceeds are received tax free. Unfortunately, the truth is that they are received free of income tax, but not free of estate tax. (If you have a large estate and a lot of life insurance you may need an Insurance Trust, but more on that later.) Once you have estimated the value of all your assets and the death benefit on your life insurance, deduct your liabilities (your mortgages and other debts). You can also deduct your estimated probate fees from this figure and you'll have a good estimate of your net estate for estate tax purposes.

None of this has to be perfect. The main figures we're concerned with is whether or not your net estate is likely to be more or less than $600,000 and, if you're married, also whether or not your net estate is likely to be more or less than $1,200,000. These are the key figures for estate planning purposes.

One major complicating factor in making an estimate that will be good for the future is, of course, inflation. We have all suffered through a general inflation that has artificially raised the value of almost all of our assets, but many of us have also seen the value of our most important asset — our home — increase way out of proportion to other increases caused by inflation. If you've owned a home in the San Francisco Bay Area, for example, for a number of years, it may well be worth four or five times what you've paid for it. It's nice to be "wealthy" of course, but since your "wealth" is your home and not some excess commodity that you don't really need to have, all this price inflation has done is create a tax problem for you. All you really have is the same house you bought several years ago. Aside from improvements you've made and paid for, it hasn't changed all that much. If you sell your home to try to cash in on all this "appreciation," you're going to have an income tax problem unless you reinvest in another property of at least equal value. If you pass your home on to your heirs at your death, you can create both

Chapter 1

Why Do I Need an Estate Plan?

Asset Inventory Worksheet

Assets	Husband's Separate Property	Wife's Separate Property	Jointly Held Property
Home	$ _____	$ _____	$ _____
Other Real Estate	_____	_____	_____
Bank Accounts			
Other Cash Accounts (Money Market Accounts, Savings, Bonds, etc.)	_____	_____	_____
Stocks, Bonds, Mutual Funds	_____	_____	_____
Business Interests	_____	_____	_____
Retirement Plan Accounts (IRAs, Keoghs, 401Ks, Pension and Profit Sharing Plans)	_____	_____	_____
Collectibles (fine art, coins, etc.)	_____	_____	_____
Personal Property	_____	_____	_____
Trusts, Annuities and other assets	_____	_____	_____
Death Benefit of Life Insurance	_____	_____	_____
Total Assets	$ _____	$ _____	$ _____
Liabilities			
Mortgages	$ _____	$ _____	$ _____
Life Insurance Loans	_____	_____	_____
Other Loans or Debts	_____	_____	_____
Total Liabilities	$ _____	$ _____	$ _____
Net Estate (Assets Less Liabilities)	$ _____	$ _____	$ _____

Why Do I Need an Estate Plan?

income tax and estate tax problems for your heirs <u>unless</u> you plan your estate properly. The government has made your home a "tax-trap."

As we stated earlier, at seven percent inflation, the value of your assets will double every ten years. Keep this in mind when trying to determine your probable net estate at the time of death.

The second important point about estate taxes that you should keep in mind is that planning will in most cases save more for married people than it will for single people. We know you single people may be wondering why we made you read through so much of this section without telling you this first. There are two good reasons. First, some of you single people may marry or remarry. Second, if one or both of your parents is alive and married (even if they are no longer married to your other natural parent) this section is still of vital importance to you. It is almost always the <u>children</u> who bear the burden of the estate tax. We know it is often delicate for children to raise this with their parents, but if your parents have not done their estate planning they may be <u>unintentionally</u> disinheriting you from a large portion of what they intended to leave you. An uncle gets the money instead — Uncle Sam. Talk to your parents. If they haven't done anything yet,

you might be able to help them organize their estate so you'll understand it and then have them make proper plans. If you find this difficult to discuss with your parents, you might consider giving them a copy of this book.

Back to the principles you need to understand about proper estate tax planning. The third point you should know is that if you leave everything to your spouse, there are no estate taxes to pay on the death of the first to die. This is called the "unlimited marital deduction." Everything is deferred to the death of the second spouse. In most cases, it is the children who bear the burden of estate taxes, not the spouse.

The fourth point you need to know about estate taxes is that everyone is allowed a $600,000 exemption. The first $600,000 of your net estate passes tax free. The key to estate planning at the estate tax level is to preserve the full $600,000 exemption for each spouse so that a married couple will be able to pass as much as $1,200,000 to their heirs tax free. <u>If you don't do any estate planning, you will lose the second $600,000 exemption</u>.

Stated another way, if you are married and you think your net estate (including the death benefit on your life insurance policies) will exceed $600,000 at the death of the <u>second</u> spouse (re-

Chapter 1

Why Do I Need an Estate Plan?

membering inflation), then you <u>must</u> do some estate planning or you will be cheating your children or other heirs out of what is rightfully theirs and you will make an unnecessary gift to the federal government. Federal estate taxes begin at 37% and go as high as 55%.

The following table sets forth the estate taxes that are payable on some amounts in excess of $600,000.

Taxable Estate	Federal Estate Tax
$ 600,000	$ -0-
750,000	55,500
850,000	94,500
1,000,000	153,000
2,000,000	255,500

For a complete estate tax chart and more examples take a look at Appendix D at the back of this book.

Attorneys who set up estate plans to minimize estate taxes by taking advantage of the unlimited marital deduction use one of two basic devices. Either they use a will with a testamentary trust or a Living Trust with a pour-over will. As we have already stated, the Living Trust avoids probate, so some attorneys will advise use of a will with a testamentary trust in order to preserve their probate fees on your death. However, if done properly, both the testamentary trust and the Living Trust will work equally well to minimize or eliminate (depending on the size of your estate) estate taxes.

There are many kinds of trusts. In Chapter 5 we will go into greater detail on exactly what a trust is. For purposes of this discussion, you need to know that there are three basic forms of estate tax minimization trusts (each one can be part of either a testamentary trust or a Living Trust). Estate planning attorneys commonly call these: (1) the A Trust; (2) the A-B Trust; and (3) the A-B-C Trust. Just to confuse things, the A Trust is sometimes called the Surviving Spouse's Trust or the Marital Trust. The B Trust is sometimes called the Decedent Spouse's Trust or the Family Trust or the By-Pass Trust. The C Trust is sometimes called a Q-Tip Trust (for Qualified Terminable Interest Property Trust). There are also other names used for the same trusts. If you get enough lawyers, congressmen and IRS types together, they'll come up with sufficient terminology to keep you confused just long enough that you may not notice that you're getting poorer and poorer. Just to attempt to keep things understandable for a change, we're going to consistently use the terms A Trust, A-B Trust and A-B-C Trust. For your convenience, we've included a glossary of many commonly used estate planning terms in Appendix H at the back of the book.

The A Trust is used for: (1) all single people; and (2) most married couples whose net estate (including life insurance death benefits) is not expected to exceed $600,000 at the death of the second spouse to die.

The A-B Trust is used for: (1) some married couples whose net estate is not expected to exceed $600,000 at the death of the second spouse; (2) most married couples whose net estate is expected to be between $600,000 and $1,200,000 at the death of the second spouse; and (3) most married couples whose net estate is expected to exceed $1,200,000 at the death of the second spouse.

The A-B-C Trust is used for some married couples whose net estate is expected to exceed $1,200,000 at the death of the first spouse.

If you have only an A Trust, it means that because you're single or because you're married and you do not expect your net estate to exceed $600,000 at the death of the second spouse to die, you do not need to worry about estate tax minimization. (Single people with estates over $600,000 need to use other estate planning devices that we'll discuss later.) We will discuss the A Trust later in Chapter 5 and not here because an A Trust is really not an inheritance tax avoidance mechanism. Its main function is to avoid probate, but when incorporated into your Living Trust it will still be the centerpiece of your Complete Estate Plan.

The purpose of the A-B Trust is to divide the joint estate of a married couple into two parts at the death of the first spouse to die. Until that first death everything is in the same trust. The division only takes place at the time of the first death. At that time, as long as the net estate is worth less than $1,200,000, one-half of the net estate will go into the A Trust, which is the surviving spouse's trust, and the other one-half of the net estate will go into the B Trust, which is the decedent spouse's trust. It may be easier for you to remember that the A Trust is for the <u>A</u>live spouse and the B Trust is for the <u>B</u>uried spouse. The A Trust remains revocable, which means that the surviving spouse can change beneficiaries at any time. The B Trust becomes irrevocable, which means that the surviving spouse can use the assets during his or her lifetime, but cannot change the ultimate beneficiaries the decedent spouse has chosen.

It is the B Trust that theoretically is being taxed on the death of the first spouse to die. But since the total estate was worth no more than $1,200,000, the amount in the B Trust will always be no more than $600,000 and thereafter will forever be exempt from estate taxes. If you have appreciating assets, such as real estate or stocks, it might be wise to place them in the B Trust. Even if the B Trust grows in value way beyond the $600,000 after the death of the first spouse to die, it will not be subject to additional estate tax when it ultimately goes to the children after the second spouse dies. But remember, you don't have to make those decisions when you set up the trust. You only allocate the assets in the trust to the A Trust and the B Trust after the first spouse dies.

When the second spouse dies, the A Trust is then subject to estate taxes, but the second $600,000 exemption is available. By using the A-B Trust, you have sheltered up to $1,200,000 from estate taxes. If you do not use the A-B Trust, a married couple will only be able to shelter a maximum of $600,000 from estate taxes if the surviving spouse is to inherit the entire estate.

Why does the government make you go through this to get your maximum benefit? A very good question. We wish we had a good answer. All we can tell you is that it's the law whether any of us like it or not, and if you don't set up an A-B Trust in this situation you are robbing your children and making a gift to the federal government.

What if your net estate is estimated to be worth more than $1,200,000 at the death of the second spouse? First we need to analyze why it is worth more than $1,200,000. If it is insurance death benefits that are pushing you significantly over the $1,200,000 mark, you may be a candidate for an Insurance Trust. This could remove the insurance death benefits from the computation of your net estate. We will discuss the Insurance Trust in greater detail in Chapter 7.

For the moment, let's assume that your net estate will probably exceed $1,200,000 at the death of the second spouse and insurance death benefits are insignificant. Your estate will be subjected to estate taxes on the death of the second spouse even with good estate planning. All we can shelter is $1,200,000. But remember if the B Trust had most of the appreciating assets in it, the children may well receive more than $1,200,000 in assets on the death of the second spouse because the B Trust was already theoretically subject to tax on the death of the first spouse and enjoyed the full $600,000 exemption. The B Trust will not be taxed again on the death of the second spouse.

If you have an A-B Trust and your net estate exceeds $1,200,000 on the death of the first spouse, only $600,000 should be allocated to the B Trust and the remainder should all be allocated to the A Trust. If you allocate more than $600,000 to the B Trust, the excess will be subject to estate taxes at the death of the first spouse, defeating your goal of deferring taxes as far into the future as possible.

So what's wrong with having more than half of the net estate in the A Trust? For most people, nothing at all. For most people an A-B Trust works well whether or not their estate exceeds $1,200,000. However, if the two spouses have different ideas on the ultimate disposition of their estate, then the A-B Trust will not give maximum protection to the first spouse to die. This most commonly occurs when one or both of the spouses has children by a prior marriage. The step-children may not be the natural objects of the bounty of the step-parent.

Remember, only the B Trust becomes irrevocable on the first death in an A-B Trust. This means that the first spouse to die can be certain that those he or she has designated will get what's left in the B Trust after the surviving spouse dies, but he or she cannot be certain that the surviving spouse will not change the beneficiaries of the A Trust.

This all works out fine if the net estate is worth less than $1,200,000 because the A Trust and the B Trust will start out equal, and it's only fair that the first spouse to die should only control the ultimate disposition of one-half of the estate. But if the net estate is over $1,200,000 there will be more in the A Trust than in the B Trust. If there is any concern that the surviving spouse may not treat the objects of the decedent spouse's bounty the way he or she might have wanted, then the parties should consider the A-B-C Trust.

In the A-B-C Trust, one-half of the estate at the time of death of the first spouse goes in the A Trust, $600,000 of the estate goes in the B Trust and the balance goes in the C Trust. Both the B Trust and the C Trust become irrevocable on the death of the first spouse to die. There are still no taxes to pay on the death of the first spouse to die because the C Trust is a special trust under the tax laws (remember, the Q-Tip Trust). If we had put more than $600,000 in the B Trust to get an equal division, it would have been taxed on the death of the first spouse.

What have we accomplished under the A-B-C Trust that we couldn't under the A-B Trust? The first spouse to die now controls the ultimate disposition of half of the net estate at the time of the death of the first spouse, not just $600,000 worth. There are some disadvantages of the A-B-C Trust which we will go into

Chapter 1

Why Do I Need an Estate Plan?

Summary of Important Estate Tax Rules

- Estate taxes are computed on net and not gross estate.

- Death benefits of life insurance policies may be included in taxable estate for estate tax purposes.

- Married couples have more opportunities to use estate planning to save estate taxes than unmarried people.

- If you leave everything to your spouse, there are no estate taxes when the first spouse dies.

- Everyone is allowed a $600,000 exemption.

- Married couples will lose the second $600,000 exemption if everything is left to the surviving spouse and they have not done any estate planning.

later. It should only be used in certain special situations. Take a look at Appendix E at the back of the book. It contains a good comparison of the A-B Trust and the A-B-C Trust.

There is a complication that we should discuss at this point. In the above discussion, we have assumed that all of the married couple's property is either community property or other jointly owned property. What about separate property?

First, let us give you a simple definition of separate and community property. Remember, this is a simple definition; there may be complexities. What else would divorce lawyers do if they couldn't argue about the complexities of our community property laws? They might have to find honest work. (We know that was a cheap shot, but still . . .)

The law <u>simply</u> stated is that separate property is the property you owned before you got married plus anything that was given to you or you inherited since your marriage and any income you receive from that property. Everything else you own is community property. Separate property can be turned into community property by making a gift to your spouse or by mixing it up with community property so that it can't easily be traced back to its separate property origins. That is the law of community

property in less than one page. For purposes of this book, it's good enough. If you're thinking about getting divorced, you'll learn a lot more about the subject before it's over.

The refinement that you need to be aware of for purposes of this book is that if one or both of the spouses has separate property at the death of the first spouse to die, the A-B Trust allocation is all of the separate property of the decedent spouse plus one-half of the community property (up to $600,000) goes in the B Trust and all of the separate property of the surviving spouse plus the balance of the community property goes in the A Trust. As you can see, this can make your estate planning more interesting. It is vital to all estate planning that you keep a separate inventory of each spouse's separate property and also the couple's community property. More on this later.

That was a short summary of what we think you need to know about the basics of estate tax avoidance. We will go into more detail on how these various trusts work in later chapters.

Avoiding Death Income Tax

What is the death income tax? It is the tax that is imposed when any heir, including the surviving spouse, sells an inherited asset. It is commonly called a

Chapter 1

Why Do I Need an Estate Plan?

capital gains tax, but at the date this book is being written, capital gains tax rates are the same as the tax rates on ordinary income. There is currently a move in Congress to reduce capital gains tax rates, but we have no way of knowing whether or not it will pass, what the rates might be if it does pass or what the rules might be in order to be able to take advantage of the lower rates.

Rest assured, however, that no matter what the fate of the current proposal to reduce the capital gains tax rate, there still will be some sort of a tax on capital gains and, therefore, there will still be a death income tax.

The death income tax is computed on the gain when the asset is sold. The gain is the net sales price less adjusted basis. Adjusted basis basically is what was originally paid for the property adjusted by certain allowable items, such as the cost of certain improvements on a home, for example.

Say, for instance, that you purchased 100 shares of stock for $10 a share ten years ago. Your adjusted basis will be $1,000. You made a good investment and you now sell your stock for $100 a share, net of commissions. Your net sales price is $10,000. Your gain is your net sales price of $10,000 less your adjusted basis of $1,000, which equals $9,000. A capital gains tax will be imposed on the $9,000. Current rates are 15%, 28% and 33%, depending on your bracket. The State of California will also charge you up to 9.3%.

There are special rules regarding the sale of your home. Assume you purchased your home fifteen years ago for $100,000. You made improvements over the years of $50,000 that are allowed to be added to your basis, so your adjusted basis is $150,000. You sell your home for $300,000 net of costs of sale. Your gain is the net sales price of $300,000 less the adjusted basis of $150,000, which equals $150,000.

This is the same as for the stock so far. However, if the sale of your home took place after either you or your spouse has reached age 55 or more, and you have occupied the house as your principal residence for three out of the last five years, the government gives you a one-time credit of $125,000. If you qualify, instead of paying taxes on $150,000 in our example, you would only pay taxes on $25,000. Remember, this is a once-in-a-lifetime exemption. Once either spouse uses it, it is lost forever for both spouses.

The other special rule relating to homes that you're probably familiar with is your ability to defer taxes on the sale of a home by purchasing another home of equal or greater value within two years from the date of sale of the first home.

Theoretically, this can be done indefinitely as long as you continue to "buy up." That is, you must always be buying houses of equal or greater value than the last home. This works fine in your early years, but may not help when your children leave home or you want to retire and move to a smaller, less expensive home. Suddenly, you're faced with the prospect of "buying-down" and paying taxes on the sale of your home.

Also, remember, this is a tax <u>deferral</u> device, not a tax <u>avoidance</u> device. This is because no matter what you have paid for each subsequent home, your basis remains what you paid for your first home. This is adjusted for allowable improvements, of course, but eventually you will be taxed on all your gain (less the one-time $125,000 exemption if you qualify) when you either choose to buy-down or choose not to buy another residence at all — or because your economic situation makes these choices for you.

The unbelievable inflation in the price of homes we have experienced in the last several years makes this an especially cruel tax. Many of us find ourselves living in homes we could no longer afford to buy at current prices. It's the same old house. You've improved it a little, but not all that much. If you sell it, you still need a place to live and <u>all</u> houses in the area are now outrageously priced.

It's not as though you purchased something special like a stock that out-performed everything else and gave you a tidy profit. You purchased a basic commodity — shelter. You still need it, but if you sell your home and cannot afford to buy another of equal or greater value, you will be faced with a tax that could force you to buy-down even more than you wanted to.

This problem is even more tragic if the sale of the home is caused by the death of a spouse. With all the other trauma occasioned by the death of a spouse, this is the worst possible time to have to face a huge tax bill.

Fortunately, the federal government has done something to help, but as usual, you have to do some planning to take full advantage of the benefit. <u>Part</u> of the benefit is automatic, but you will lose the <u>full</u> benefit if you haven't planned properly.

The benefit is called "stepped-up basis." Upon death, your adjusted basis of any asset (not just your home) becomes its fair market value at the date of your death. This means that if the asset is sold shortly after your death, there probably will be no death income tax at all. Even if it is not sold shortly after your death, your heirs will <u>never</u> be taxed on the gains before your death. For example, you purchased stock for

Chapter 1

Why Do I Need an Estate Plan?

$1,000 which was worth $10,000 when you die. The stock is left to your children who hold it for a few years and then sell it at $15,000. The tax will be on the $5,000 gain after your death. The $9,000 gained during your lifetime will never be taxed.

So what's the problem? The problem is that for married couples, the stepped-up basis will apply only to one-half of the gain on the death of the first spouse to die if you've planned incorrectly, but it will apply to all of the gain if you've planned correctly. This is what we mean by elimination of the death income tax by proper planning.

Let's imagine two couples with identical situations, except for their estate planning. They both purchased homes in 1960 for $100,000 and both made $50,000 in allowable improvements over the years. They were "lucky" and bought their homes next door to each other in the San Francisco Bay Area, where real estate agents will tell you about the fantastic "appreciation" in the value of their houses. Our couples didn't really feel any richer. They were still living in the same houses they bought in 1960, but their net worth just kept growing — on paper at least. In 1990 both houses were worth $600,000 and the mortgages were finally paid. Unfortunately both husbands died early in the year. (We sus-

pect that making the last mortgage payment was just too much of a shock for them.) Both widows are over 55 and want to sell their homes to move into smaller condos.

As you might guess, Couple A planned their estate and Couple B did not. We aren't going to go into all of the problems of Widow B here, just the death income taxes, but remember, death income taxes will be only one of the many problems she will face because of her failure to plan her estate.

Because Couple A planned their estate properly (we will show you how in Chapter 2), Widow A sells her home without payment of any death income taxes. She has $600,000 in the bank. She can purchase her new condo outright, with no mortgage payment, have money in the bank and still not have used her $125,000 one-time tax exemption. If she ever sells the condo for a gain, she still has her $125,000 exemption available.

Widow B finds herself in a much different situation. No planning or poor planning allows her to only have one-half of the step-up in basis. The original basis was $150,000 and the net sale price was $600,000, for a gain of $450,000. There is a step-up because of her husband's death of one-half of the gain or $225,000. When she sells the home she

Why Do I Need an Estate Plan?

Couple A (Proper planning)

Original basis	$150,000
Stepped-up basis	$600,000
Net sales price	$600,000
Less basis	-$600,000
Taxable gain	-0-

Net result: No death income tax and $125,000 exemption not used.

Couple B (Improper or no planning)

Original basis	$150,000
Stepped-up basis	$225,000
Net sales price	$600,000
Less basis	-$375,000
Gain	$225,000
Exemption	-$125,000
Taxable gain	$100,000
Death income tax	$ 33,000

Net result: $33,000 in death income tax and permanent loss of $125,000 exemption.

Chapter 1

Why Do I Need an Estate Plan?

faces taxes on $225,000. She can of course use her $125,000 one-time exemption and reduce the gain to $100,000. (Remember, this only works for your residence. There is no such exemption for other assets.) Widow B will probably have about $33,000 less to spend on her condo than Widow A <u>and</u> she will have lost the right to use the $125,000 exemption when she sells the condo.

Widow B has made a $33,000 gift to the federal government. She would be making an even larger gift if for some reason the $125,000 exemption were not available to her.

Why does the government penalize her for improper planning? Again, we don't know why, but we do know that if you don't get actively involved in protecting yourself and your family, you will be forced into accepting the plan the government has for you.

Avoidance of Conservatorship

Because we are living longer, even the healthiest of us faces the increased risk of mental or physical incapacity, either permanent or temporary. The fastest growing segment of our population is people over age 85. There are over 25,000 Americans now over 100 years of age. Almost all of us want to live to an advanced age (given the alternative, who wouldn't?). Unfortunately, as healthier lifestyles and medical advances allow more and more of us to live longer and longer, we are faced with mounting problems of more and more people who become incapacitated and unable to manage their own affairs.

When we are no longer capable of dealing with our assets, the law requires our relatives or friends to petition the Probate Court for the appointment of a conservator of our assets. Nothing that is processed through the legal system is simple, inexpensive or private. Conservatorship proceedings are no exception. In fact, because of the nature of having to deal with the affairs of an incapacitated person, these proceedings are often particularly embarrassing, time consuming and expensive.

As a result of conservatorship proceedings, detailed records of every transaction must be kept and annual accountings filed with Probate Court. Most conservators find it necessary to hire accountants and lawyers to conduct business and run personal affairs that they were able to handle on their own before their lives became public business.

Conservatorship is a growing problem. It is estimated that approximately two-thirds of all proceedings before the California Probate Courts are now conservatorship proceedings instead of probates.

Traditional estate planning, with wills and testamentary trusts, doesn't even deal with this problem. It is only concerned about what happens after death.

If you have a properly written Living Trust, however, the whole conservatorship problem can be avoided. The Living Trust is the only estate planning vehicle that deals with this problem, because it is the only estate planning vehicle that is in effect during your lifetime.

We'll give you more information on how the Living Trust works in avoiding conservatorship later on.

The Government Plan

Before we go on to the various ways you can get involved in your estate plan, let's review the plan the government has for you by measuring it against our estate planning goals.

- <u>Choice of heirs</u>. You get no choice. Take a look at the government's choices for your estate in Appendix A at the back of this book. If that's exactly what you want for your estate, fine. If not, get involved and make your own choice.

- <u>Probate</u>. Since you don't have a will, there is no will to probate. But don't get excited, the government plan for the administration of intestate (no will)

estates is just as bad as the probate process.

- <u>Estate taxes</u>. You will pay the maximum allowed.

- <u>Death income taxes</u>. You will pay the maximum allowed.

- <u>Conservatorship</u>. If you or your spouse should become incapacitated, the government plan involves time, expense, lawyers, courts and publicity, all of which could have been avoided with proper planning.

- <u>Control over assets</u>. Control over your own assets stops upon incapacity or death of first spouse.

- <u>Flexibility</u>. Flexibility stops upon incapacity or death of first spouse.

- <u>Privacy</u>. Privacy stops upon incapacity or death of first spouse.

- <u>Health care</u>. You may find yourself or your spouse hooked up to various life sustaining machines against your will for months or even years, resulting in both untold agony and bankruptcy.

- <u>Funeral and burial instructions</u>. You have added to your family's trauma at

Chapter 1

Why Do I Need an Estate Plan?

The Government's Will

Since the Deceased was unwilling to spend the time and effort to plan his estate, the State of California makes the following provisions for his family:

- Deceased's widow receives all of the couple's community property, but only 1/3 of Deceased's separate property. The other 2/3 of Deceased's separate property goes to Deceased's three children in equal shares.
- Deceased's widow shall administer the estate, subject to the scrutinty and control of the Probate Court.
- Deceased's widow shall be custodian of the assets of the children until they reach majority, at which time they may sue her for mismanaging their funds.
- If Deceased's widow dies with as little planning as Deceased, the Probate Court will select the guardian for the children.
- Deceased's widow may remarry and disinherit the children.
- The government gets to charge the estate with all taxes at the maximum allowable rate, with no effort to reduce taxes.
- The government gets to decide what the attorney's fees will be for handling the estate.
- The estate shall remain open for as long as the Probate Court thinks it's desirable.
- Friends, neighbors, business competitors, creditors, etc. are all invited to take a look at the Deceased's family affairs anytime they choose.
- If the children do end up with any money, they get it all at age 18, free of any restrictions of any kind.
- MAY HE REST IN PEACE!

the time of your death. You could have relieved them of these decisions. Moreover, your own personal wishes may not be known and never be followed.

- <u>Anatomical gifts</u>. There will probably be none, even if you would have wanted to make a gift.

- <u>Administration of estate</u>. You have made the administration of your estate as slow, expensive and difficult as possible.

We know that if you're interested enough to be reading this book, none of you would want this result. My job in writing this book is to get you motivated to do something to help yourself and your family. You have an opportunity to do something now. Most of us miss our opportunities because they come to us disguised as work. The problem is that you don't know exactly <u>what</u> to do; you're concerned about how much time and effort it will take to plan your estate; you're concerned about who to have help you with the technical aspects of planning your estate and you're concerned about the cost of planning your estate. The balance of this book will attempt to show you that what most of you need to do is to establish a Complete Estate Plan using the Living Trust and that if

you have competent professionals assisting you, it will be relatively easy and surprisingly inexpensive.

This will be the best present you can give to yourself and your family. You and your family may well save thousands of dollars in probate costs and taxes and you will have the peace of mind in knowing that you, and not the government, have made the decisions on how you and your family are going to be treated on your death or incapacity.

Chapter 2
What's Wrong with Joint Tenancy?

There are many legal forms two or more people may use to own property together: partnerships, trusts, corporations, community property, tenancy in common, tenancy by the entirety, joint tenancy, etc. Since this is not a book for law students, we won't bore you with the history and technicalities of each form of ownership.

Many of you are aware of joint tenancy, because that's the way you hold much of your property. You hold it that way either because you believe that you will avoid probate that way, and that that's all the estate planning you need, or because when you bought your house the title company suggested you take title that way, or maybe some combination of being told to do it that way and thinking that you've solved your estate planning problems with no effort and at no expense.

Joint tenancy means that two or more people own property together and that the survivor will own the property at the death of the other or others, without probate and even in disregard of a will. Even if you attempt to give joint tenancy property to someone else in your will, it will have no effect. No probate is necessary because title vests in the surviving joint tenant automatically as a property right.

Sounds pretty good so far. But most people who own property together as joint tenants are husband and wife. When the first spouse dies, there is no probate, but when the second spouse dies, there is no other joint tenant and probate then becomes necessary.

The answer, it would seem, would be to add an adult child as a joint tenant either while both parents are alive or certainly after the first dies. This does avoid the probate on the estate of the second to die, but also creates two major problems. First, the additional joint tenant or tenants will become your heir

Chapter 2

What's Wrong with Joint Tenancy?

or heirs as to that asset. This works fine if you want to leave that asset to your only child, who is an adult and lives nearby. If you want the asset to go to more than one person, they all have to be joint tenants. As a practical matter, all joint tenants have to be adults and have to be easily available to sign all documents relating to the asset.

The second major problem of adding someone other than your spouse as a joint tenant to your property is that they immediately become a co-owner of the property. This means that your property is now subject to the claims of your co-owner's creditors. Is your child in business? Just about any business can have financial problems and, at worst, face bankruptcy. Is your child a professional? Almost all professionals face mounting problems with malpractice suits, sometimes beyond insurance limits. (We know your son, the doctor, is careful, but these days, in our litigious society, that's often not enough.) Does your child drive a car? One serious accident beyond insurance limits could imperil your joint tenancy property.

Another problem with joint tenancy in some situations is that the first to die loses total control over the ultimate disposition of the entire asset on the death of the second spouse. Many of us have children by a prior marriage that we

want to provide for if our spouse does not use up the entire estate. You can't do this with joint tenancy. The surviving spouse may leave the entire asset to his or her children by a prior marriage. This is not the case with a Living Trust, where the first to die can make certain that on the death of the surviving spouse his or her half of any or all assets passes to the heirs he or she selected. Joint tenancy is like using an axe instead of a scalpel in this situation.

All this aside, however, the biggest single reason to avoid joint tenancy is to avoid death income taxes. If you and your spouse hold any property as joint tenants at the time of the death of the first to die, only one-half of the value of the property will have the benefit of the step-up in basis. The step-up in basis is one of the most important benefits found anywhere in our tax codes and you will have given half of that benefit away by holding your property in joint tenancy. Why is this so? Just because that's the way the law is written. It's not fair, but it's what we have to live with. It makes joint tenancy one of the worst ways for you to hold your property.

One of the most important features of the Complete Estate Plan is to have all married couples terminate their joint tenancies and convert their property to community property inside the Living

Trust. Community property gets a 100% step-up in basis, instead of the 50% step-up in basis for joint tenancy property. The Living Trust avoids probate, which is what you wanted from the joint tenancy in the first place, it distributes your asset to your desired heirs at your death without the risks of co-ownership during your lifetime and, by calling the asset community property, it gives you 100% of the advantages of a stepped-up basis.

Let's take a look at the differing results in a simple situation. Twenty years ago a husband and wife started a small business with little or no capital, but built it up with "sweat equity" — hard work. Early on they incorporated their business and their lawyer put title in the name of husband and wife, as joint tenants, on the stock certificate in order to avoid probate. His heart was in the right place, but he either did not know about Living Trusts (surprisingly, many lawyers do not) or thought the estate was just too small at the time to bother. The stock certificate was tucked away with the corporate records and kept in the lawyer's office. Our couple never considered selling the business so no one ever took another look at the certificate.

Twenty years later, the husband dies and the business passes directly to his widow without the time and expense of probate. The family lawyer is looking good at this point (unless, of course, the rest of couple's assets had to be probated). The widow decides that she does not want to run the family business and sells it for $1,000,000. Her lawyer explains that she is lucky because her death income tax is so low. Since the original basis of the stock was close to zero (remember, they started the business with little or no capital), her gain would have been close to $1,000,000 had the stock been sold during the joint lifetime of husband and wife. But because of the step-up in basis on the husband's death, one-half of the value of the property is stepped up to its value on the date of the husband's death. Therefore, the new basis is $500,000 instead of zero and the taxable gain is only $500,000 and not $1,000,000. A death tax of only approximately $165,000 is due (assuming a 33% bracket) instead of approximately $330,000.

Everything the lawyer has told the widow is true, but sadly, the widow has just made an unnecessary gift to the federal government of $165,000, plus another gift to the state government in an amount that varies depending on which state she lives in (up to 9.3% in California).

At any time before the death of the husband the couple could have very sim-

Chapter 2

What's Wrong with Joint Tenancy?

ply created a Living Trust and transferred the family business corporate stock to the name of the Living Trust, changing the character of the stock from joint tenancy to community property. Still no probate when the husband dies, but this time, when the widow sells her stock there is no death income tax at all. The step-up in basis is 100% of the value of the stock at the date of husband's death. The widow could have saved over $165,000 in taxes at a probable cost of around $1,000 to do a Complete Estate Plan with a Living Trust. (More on costs of setting up a plan later.)

Our example gets worse, of course, because when the widow passes away, her entire estate is probated, at great time and expense, and because even after death income taxes were paid her estate still exceeded $600,000, and as she and her husband had never set up an A-B Trust, her children will now be saddled with unnecessary estate taxes.

Each and every one of this unfortunate family's problems was avoidable. There could have been no death income taxes, there could have been no probate fees, there could have been no delay in passing the estate to the children and there could have been no estate taxes.

Did joint tenancy solve their problems or cause them? The real culprit is not joint tenancy; the real problem is lack of planning. Joint tenancy sounds easy and inexpensive. It is easy and inexpensive in the beginning, but it is likely to be anything but easy and inexpensive later on down the road.

A word here — slightly out of place — about separate property. We bring up separate property ownership here because it shares one of the problems of joint tenancy property — failure to take advantage of the step-up in basis. Simply stated, separate property is property that you owned prior to your marriage or that was given to you or that you inherited, that you have not commingled with your community property. In order to get the full advantage of the stepped-up basis rules, the property must be community property and not separate property, even in your Living Trust. A Living Trust allows you to continue to hold your property as either separate property or community property or to change any separate property to community property. If you convert your separate property to community property, it will enjoy the full step-up in basis upon the death of either spouse.

For example, a wife owns $100,000 in stock with a $20,000 basis that she received from a divorce settlement from her prior marriage. When she remarries, she keeps this stock as her separate property. On the death of her sec-

What's Wrong with Joint Tenancy?

Step-up in Basis Depends on how Married Couple Holds Title to Property

Community Property

Husband dies	100%
Wife dies	100%

Joint Tenancy

Husband dies	50%
Wife dies	50%

Tenants in Common

Husband dies	50%
Wife dies	50%

Husband's Separate Property

Husband dies	100%
Wife dies	NONE

Wife's Separate Property

Husband dies	NONE
Wife dies	100%

ond husband, she has no step-up in basis. When she sells the stock, she has a taxable gain of $80,000. Had she converted the stock to community property, she would have had the benefit of the full step-up in basis and there would have been no capital gains tax on the sale of the stock. (All of our examples assume that the sale takes place shortly after the death of the spouse and that there is no change in value from the date of death to the date of sale. If there is an increase in the value after the date of death, you are only taxed on the amount of that increase.)

A word of caution, however. Conversion of separate property to community property involves a gift of one-half of that property to your spouse. This means that if you should divorce, your spouse will be entitled to one-half of the value of that property instead of none of it. It also means that your spouse will have the right to control the disposition of one-half of its value on his or her death instead of none of it.

Conversion of <u>separate</u> property to community property should be done only after a careful consideration of all of its consequences. In situations involving prior marriages, many people want to use their separate property to separately provide for their children by a prior marriage. Conversion of <u>joint</u> <u>tenancy</u>

property to community property, however, should be done in <u>every</u> circumstance as long as its done in a Living Trust to continue to avoid probate.

Now that we've gotten ourselves back to our original subject — joint tenancy — let's review how many of our original estate planning goals are achieved using joint tenancy:

- <u>Choice of heirs</u>. Joint tenancy works fine as long as your heir is your spouse. You get into trouble when it's anyone else because you've given them <u>current</u> co-ownership with you instead of delaying their ownership until after your death. This means they can use the property just as you can, and it means that their creditors can reach your property to satisfy their debts. Also, every time any documents regarding the property need to be signed, they will have to be signed by all owners (except in the case of joint bank accounts). Simply stated, you have lost the exclusive control and enjoyment of the property.

- <u>Probate</u>. Since joint tenancy avoids probate, this is viewed as its single greatest, and perhaps only, virtue. For married couples, of course, it only avoids probate of the estate of the first to die. Unless the surviving spouse forms a new joint tenancy with the ultimate heirs, with all of the problems we've outlined above, the entire estate must be probated on the death of the second to die.

- Estate taxes. Joint tenancy does nothing to help you avoid estate taxes. You will pay the maximum allowed.

- Death income taxes. This is where joint tenancy really fails you. The surviving spouse will pay the maximum allowed.

- Conservatorship. Joint tenancy does nothing to avoid conservatorships. Since all co-owners are required to act with regard to the property, if any co-owner becomes incapacitated, a conservatorship will have to be established (except for bank accounts). Joint tenancy may increase your chances of having to be involved with a conservatorship because more people are involved if your co-owner is anyone other than your spouse.

- Control over assets. This is a substantial disadvantage unless your only joint tenant is your spouse. You have given away valuable property rights now instead of after your death. You no longer have the right to exclusive control and enjoyment. Moreover, joint tenancy limits the control the first spouse to die has over the distribution of assets upon the death of the surviving spouse.

- Flexibility. Joint tenancy with your spouse is flexible. You can still establish a Living Trust and convert the property to community property. Joint tenancy with anyone other than your spouse is extremely inflexible. You have given away property rights that you can't get back unless the other person is willing to give them back.

- Privacy. Joint tenancy works much better than probate in preserving privacy, but the Living Trust works just as well.

- Health care. If you own all your property in joint tenancy, you may mistakenly believe that you've done all the estate planning you need to do. Not only have you done a poor job, you've done an incomplete job. A Complete Estate Plan takes into account planning for all aspects of death or incapacity. If you find yourself in the tragic situation of having your spouse's life artificially sustained when he or she can no longer participate in decisions, whom do you want to make the deci-

Chapter 2

What's Wrong with Joint Tenancy?

Advantages and Disadvantages of Joint Tenancy

Advantages

- Simple.
- Inexpensive.
- Avoids probate on first death.

Disadvantages

- Loss of complete step-up in basis.
- Loss of exclusive control.
- Subjects asset to creditors of joint tenants.
- Does not avoid probate on death of last joint tenant.
- Cannot delay distribution to survivor.
- May pass property to unintended heirs.
- Subjects asset to conservatorship.
- May increase estate taxes for married couple with more than $600,000 in net assets.

---

sions, yourself or the government?

• <u>Funeral and burial instructions</u>. Joint tenancy only decides how your property is to be distributed at your death. It is not a Complete Estate Plan. You have done nothing to relieve your survivors of the burden of these decisions.

• <u>Anatomical gifts</u>. No, you can't put your heart in joint tenancy. If you do want to make an anatomical gift you have to do more than just keeping your property in joint tenancy.

• <u>Administration of estate</u>. To the extent that you have avoided probate, you have substantially eased the administration of your estate. To the extent that you have forgotten to put any assets in joint tenancy, you may still have to face probate. You also probably will be dealing with probate on the death of the second spouse to die. You must still terminate joint tenancies on the death of a joint tenant. You may be unpleasantly surprised at the cost and time involved in doing so.

Joint tenancy may be better than doing nothing at all, but it's not estate planning. In fact you probably already hold property in joint tenancy without being aware of it. Take a look at the deed to your house and some stock certificates. Chances are that you might find joint tenancy mentioned whether you remember it that way or not. This is planning by accident, instead of planning by making informed decisions.

As we hope we've shown you, joint tenancy is no substitute for a Complete Estate Plan with a Living Trust.

Chapter 3
What's Wrong with Giving It Away?

"It is better to give than to receive." It may seem to you that the best way to avoid probate and taxes is to give some or all of your property away before you die, but with the advent of modern tax laws, making the government our not so silent partner in every transaction, nothing is simple, not even making a gift.

If you want to make a gift to a charity, it is tax deductible as long as the charity properly qualifies with the Internal Revenue Service. If you want the tax deduction, make sure the charity is qualified. Most are, but if the charity is not well known in your community, check it out.

All other gifts are not tax deductible. In fact, if you're not careful, they may be taxable to you.

The first gift tax rule that you should be aware of is that all gifts to your spouse are tax free. As we saw earlier, you _may_ want to consider converting some or all of your separate property to community property. If you do so, one-half of the value of the property is a gift to your spouse. But since your spouse is the recipient of the gift, it is tax free. This means that you may convert as much separate property to community property as you like without being concerned with tax consequences. You do, however, have to be concerned with the non-tax consequences of the gift, such as the effects of divorce or of the death of your spouse.

The second important gift tax rule is that each of us has a lifetime exemption from gift taxes of $600,000. Each of us may give away up to $600,000 during our lifetimes without having to pay any gift taxes. The catch is that the $600,000 exemption is the exact same exemption that we have for estate taxes. It's a unified exemption, which means that certain gifts that are not taxed now reduce the estate tax exemption and will be taxed later. But a good rule about

Chapter 3

What's Wrong with Giving It Away?

taxes is better later than now. Your children, who will be making the later payment, may not agree, but they didn't argue when they got the gift, did they? Gifts are also taxed at the same rate as estates — 37% to 55%. Fortunately, there is no separate California gift tax.

The third basic rule you should know about gift taxes is that you can give up to $10,000 per year per donee with no tax consequences and without reducing your $600,000 unified estate and gift tax exemption. This means, for example, that a married couple can give up to $20,000 per child per year. We'd all like to be that child, right? Remember, since it's a gift, it's your child's separate property and not his or her community property, even if married. So you don't have to worry. If you don't like your daughter-in-law, you can still make the gift to your son.

A word of caution about the use of the $10,000 exemption if you establish a Living Trust. The current IRS position is that any gift made directly from a trust will be included in your taxable estate if you die within three years of making the gift. If you have a Living Trust and want to safely take advantage of the annual $10,000 exclusion, remove the funds from your Living Trust and place them in a bank account in your own name before you make the gift.

The fourth basic rule you should know about gift taxes is that the donee takes the donor's basis. This means that if you give your grandson stock worth $10,000 for which you paid $1,000, and he immediately sells it for $10,000 to buy a car, he has a taxable gain of $9,000 and will have to buy a much cheaper car than he wanted. If he had inherited the stock from you, he would have had a step-up in basis to the value of the stock at the date of your death, with no tax to pay if he sells at the same value. Because of the step-up in basis rules, cash is always the best gift because its basis is always its current value. Your grandson could have told you that in the first place. Also, by waiting to make the gift until you pass on, your grandson may have matured and not wasted the money on a fast car. But, maybe not.

Speaking of giving things to your grandchildren, beware of gifts of real estate. If you give real estate to your grandchildren, it will cause reassessment of the property under California's Proposition 13. This could result in disastrously higher local property taxes. Remember, on every possible transaction, there are always one or more government agencies attempting to impose a variety of taxes. You have to watch from all directions. There are more of them than there are of you.

Basis Depends on Whether Asset is Received by Gift or Inheritance

April 1, 1985 -   Grandfather buys 2,000 shares of Big Winner, Inc. for $1.00 per share.

January 1, 1990 -   Shares are worth $10.00 each. Grandfather makes an outright gift of 1,000 shares to his granddaughter and leaves the other 1,000 shares to his grandson in his will.

January 15, 1990 - Grandfather dies.

January 16, 1990 - Granddaughter and grandson both sell their shares at $10.00 per share.

Granddaughter

Net sales price	$10,000.00
Adjusted basis	-1,000.00
Taxable gain	$ 9,000.00

Grandson

Net sales price	$10,000.00
Adjusted basis	-10,000.00
Taxable gain	$ - 0 -

Chapter 3

What's Wrong with Giving It Away?

Speaking of Proposition 13, the good news is that putting your real property in your Living Trust will <u>not</u> cause a reassessment. More on that later.

Aside from all these tax rules, the real question you have to ask yourself is whether or not you really want to give your property away while you're still around to enjoy it. For some of us with sufficient assets, the answer is clearly yes. There is real pleasure in giving that may outweigh any tax considerations.

But be careful. Some of the objects of your bounty may not yet be mature enough to handle outright gifts. If this is the case, you might want to consider a special trust for this purpose. This would be in addition to your Living Trust, because a Living Trust is totally revocable during your lifetime, so you can always change your mind. If it's really a gift, you can't change your mind and take it back. You need an irrevocable Children's Trust to accomplish this purpose. The typical Children's Trust gives all income from the property held in trust to the children or grandchildren and then starts to distribute principal in increments as the children reach certain ages, such as one-third at age 25, one-third at age 30 and one-third at age 35.

You might want to consider a similar formula for distributions from your Living Trust. That way if the recipient is too immature to handle money at age 25, he or she will only lose one-third of the inheritance and, we hope, will learn something by the first mistake that will help preserve the balance of the inheritance.

Once you give a gift, you lose control of it, of course, or it's not a gift. You must be willing to accept that consequence.

Many people in businesses or professions that are at high risk to exposure to lawsuits or other creditors attempt to make themselves "judgment proof" by giving all their assets to their spouse. In order for this to work, it must truly be a transfer of ownership and it must not be a "fraud on creditors." Most states have now adopted a uniform law on fraudulent conveyances making it much easier for creditors to set aside these arrangements than in the past. If you are considering "putting it all in the wife's name," you need to get familiar with these laws as soon as possible. Moreover, be aware that if you have protected yourself against creditors by making yourself a pauper, you've put yourself at the mercy of your spouse. In case of divorce, there will be no community property to divide. It will all be your spouse's separate property. Your spouse could also completely disinherit you, leaving you with nothing on his or her death. Also, since more and more families have both spouses working and somewhat equally exposed to creditors and lawsuits, it's often difficult to see which spouse should own the property.

It is important to note that the Living Trust is <u>not</u> a device to protect you against lawsuits or creditors. It will avoid probate; it will reduce or eliminate estate taxes; it will eliminate death income taxes; and it will avoid conservatorship, but it will not shield your assets from your creditors during your lifetime. However, after the death of the first spouse, the assets in both the B Trust and the C Trust are exempt from creditors of the surviving spouse. Creditors of the surviving spouse may only attach assets in the A Trust.

Let's go through our estate planning objectives to see how well gifts work.

- <u>Choice of heirs</u>. To the extent that you've already given your property to whom you want it to go, gifts accomplish your purpose. If you don't have a will or a Living Trust and you still own property on your death, you're going to have to be content with the heirs that the government has picked out for you.

- <u>Probate</u>. If you don't own it when you die, it won't be probated. If you can reduce your <u>gross</u> estate to below $60,000 by giving the rest away during your lifetime, you may well avoid probate. This is impractical for most of us, but it could work in certain circumstances. In most other cases, the balance in your estate will still be probated.

- <u>Estate taxes</u>. To the extent that you use your $10,000 per year per donee exemption, you may reduce your net combined gift and estate taxes. However, if your net estate (including the death benefit of your life insurance) plus the gifts you've made in excess of the $10,000 exemptions still exceeds $600,000, then married couples should still have either an A-B Trust or an A-B-C Trust to minimize or eliminate estate taxes. The best way to set up either of these trusts is with a Living Trust.

- <u>Death income taxes</u>. Since the donor takes the donee's basis, gifts are as bad as joint tenancy for income tax purposes. Appreciated property is always better received by inheritance rather than by gift.

- <u>Conservatorship</u>. If you start giving it all away, you might be considered a likely candidate for a conservatorship. Seriously, a gifting program does nothing to help solve this problem. You

Chapter 3

What's Wrong with Giving It Away?

Summary of Important Gift Tax Rules

- Only gifts to qualified charities are tax deductible. Other gifts may be taxable to the donor.

- All gifts to a spouse are tax free.

- Everyone has a lifetime exemption from gift taxes of $600,000, but it's the same $600,000 exemption from estate taxes.

- You may give up to $10,000 per year per donor per donee without depleting your $600,000 lifetime exemption. Gifts from your Living Trust under this exemption should be made by transferring the funds out of the Living Trust before the gift is made.

- The donor takes the donee's basis.

- There are no separate California gift taxes.

still need a Complete Estate Plan with a Living Trust.

• <u>Control over assets</u>. If you make an <u>unrestricted</u> gift, you lose control over it immediately. There have been countless lawsuits between parents and their children (a genuine tragedy) when the parents have "given" the property to their children "with a wink" still intending to control the property. The problem arises, of course, when the children didn't understand the "wink" the same as the parents. The children now begin to exercise control over the asset and the parents try to stop them. In the modern world this means litigation. Nothing can be more destructive of the family relationship or the family fortune, large or small, than the civil litigation system as it exists today. Even the simplest lawsuits usually take years and cost tens of thousands of dollars. If you make a <u>restricted</u> gift through a Children's Trust, for example, you can exercise some control over how and when the recipients will receive their gifts.

• <u>Flexibility</u>. Gifting programs don't score high here. Once you've made your gift, it's made. If you try to take it back or exercise some control again in the future, watch out for lots of emo-

tional and financial grief. Even with a Children's Trust, you have to decide at the outset what you want. Since the trust is irrevocable, it can't be changed once it's set in place. One of the best features of the Living Trust is that it's completely revocable, meaning you can change it at any time during the joint lifetimes of its creators.

• <u>Privacy</u>. A gifting program, to the extent that it removes items from your probate estate, does preserve privacy as to those items. To the extent that you still have an estate to probate, you have lost privacy. Most of us who are well enough off to make substantial gifts during our lifetimes will still have an estate left that's large enough to probate.

• <u>Health care</u>. Since gifting is not really an estate plan, it does nothing with regard to your health care decisions.

• <u>Funeral and burial instructions</u>. Again, if you're only making gifts, you're not doing your job. You're generous, but you're forgetting to make the best gift you can — a Complete Estate Plan, which includes the gift of having made your own funeral and burial instructions.

Chapter 3

What's Wrong with Giving It Away?

- <u>Anatomical gifts</u>. In the last chapter we said that you couldn't put your heart in joint tenancy. But you can give your heart away (no, we don't mean just on Valentine's Day). We know many of you may not be interested in this program, but for those of you that are, this is a gift that could mean far more to its recipient than any financial gift you could ever make. A Complete Estate Plan at least encourages you to consider your options and not let others or inertia make the decision for you.

- <u>Administration of estate</u>. To the degree that you've given your assets away, you've made the administration of your estate simpler and less expensive. But most of us are not going to give all of it away before we go. If a probate is still going to be necessary, you haven't done the job.

As we've seen, gifting can be a <u>part</u> of your Complete Estate Plan using the Living Trust, but it is not a substitute. Give your family and yourself more than just immediate gifts. Give yourself control over your own situation. Give yourself and your family the financial benefits and peace of mind of a Complete Estate Plan using the Living Trust.

Chapter 4
What's Wrong with a Will?

A will is a written document giving directions to others on how you want your assets distributed on your death and making other appropriate directives about guardianship for your children, appointment of your executor and disposition of your remains. To the degree your will is valid, the government will enforce it.

Basically, there are two types of wills: holographic and attested.

Holographic wills are usually made without lawyers. They are wills written on plain paper (modern rules allow some printing on the paper, but don't risk it), entirely in your own handwriting (which better be legible if you want it to work), dated and signed at the bottom. As long as you can make your wishes clear (remember, lawyers and judges will be looking at your will, and they can make tap water look muddy), your holographic will will work as well as an attested will.

The attested will is what we usually think of as a will. It's usually typed and prepared by a lawyer, but not necessarily so. The main difference from a holographic will is that it must be signed in front of two witnesses (three in a few states) who do not benefit from the terms of the will.

Most people think that they need a will. Most people do not have a will. Unfortunately, the last two sentences summarize the sorry state of estate planning in this country.

If after reading this far we haven't convinced you of anything (maybe we should consider giving you a refund) and you don't have a will and think that's all you need to do, stop now and write one. Writing a holographic will will take you less time than it would take you to finish this book. If you don't want to do a holographic will and don't want to spend any money on a lawyer (a universal desire), you can send $1.00 to the California State Bar and they will give you a fill-in-the

Chapter 4

What's Wrong with a Will?

blanks form you can use.

Why is the California State Bar being so nice to you? Because wills mean probate. Lawyers don't make any money writing wills. They're loss leaders for probate fees. We know it's a waiting game, but it's the game that's played. Estate planning attorneys see file cabinets full of wills as annuities for the future.

Having a will is not planning your estate. You <u>have</u> selected your heirs, but you've robbed the very heirs you've selected of time, money and privacy by failing to have a Living Trust.

With a Living Trust, your heirs will be in full control of what you left them in a matter of hours or days at the worst. With a will, they may wait one to two years to gain control.

With a Living Trust, your heirs will gain control of what you have left them at little or no administrative cost. With a will your heirs will pay probate costs in California based on your <u>gross</u> estate as follows:

Gross Probate Estate	Statutory Fees
$ 75,000	4,800
100,000	6,300
150,000	8,300
200,000	10,300
300,000	14,300
400,000	18,300
500,000	22,300
1,000,000	42,300

With a Living Trust, your heirs will be able to operate in complete privacy, without your affairs being made part of the public record. With a will, every aspect of your estate will be a public record, which means everyone who wants to can review all of your financial affairs when either you or your spouse dies.

Possibly the worst aspect of having a will is that it lulls people into believing that they've done their job. After all, they've done more than the 70% of us who don't even have a will at all.

The problem is that attorneys are not doing their job in educating the 30% of us who come to them wanting to do something about planning our estates. It's easy to say that attorneys are not doing their job because they want the probate fees (attorneys are easy targets these days), but in many cases attorneys are not advising their clients to use Living Trusts not out of personal greed, but out of ignorance. Until recently the Living Trust was used only by the wealthy to protect very large estates. Lawyers, like everyone else, are creatures of habit. Everyone who's seen them about estate planning in the past has gotten a will; therefore, everyone will get one in the

Assets Controlled by a Will

- Assets that are separate property in your name alone.

- One-half of assets that are community property whether the property is held in both spouses' names or yours alone.

- Your interest in assets registered in your name as a tenant in common with someone else.

- Your interest in assets that are not registered, such as furniture, jewelry, bearer bonds, etc. (unless transferred to a Living Trust).

Assets Not Controlled by a Will

- Any assets transferred to a Living Trust.

- Assets held in joint tenancy.

- Life insurance benefits (unless your estate is named as beneficiary).

- Retirement plan benefits, such as IRAs, pension plans, etc. (unless your estate is named as beneficiary).

- Totten trust bank accounts.

Chapter 4

What's Wrong with a Will?

future. There's nothing a lawyer likes better than precedent. Even if he or she knows about the Living Trust, your lawyer may be uncomfortable about the fact that there are so few of them. He or she may not be aware that the Living Trust has a history going back to at least medieval times in England, that it's recognized in all fifty states and by the IRS. But your lawyer is right, there aren't very many of them. It's believed that less than 1% of the U.S. population has a Living Trust. The fact that it works very well for that 1% won't impress your lawyer if he or she doesn't know that it works so well.

What every lawyer does understand is a will. It works and it works well — for your lawyer — and not so well for you and your family, but that's the way it's expected to work. It's like having cancer. You're not expected to enjoy it.

We believe that as the word gets out, as more and more of you establish Living Trusts, as soon as people begin to realize that Living Trusts are not just for the rich, that attorneys will become more and more comfortable with the idea and will begin to be forced by the demands of their clients to learn more about the Living Trust.

A word of warning — don't be your attorney's Living Trust experiment (don't be your brain surgeon's first live patient either, or you might not be a live patient for long). It takes a lot of work to become familiar with the legal technicalities necessary to properly prepare a Living Trust. They're more complicated than a will. It then takes experience to know how to make the Living Trust work for the individual needs of each client. All Living Trusts are not the same. If an attorney were to do this for you at his or her normal hourly rate (not many attorneys charge less than $100 per hour these days), the cost would be out of your reach and you would still be getting an experiment. We know your attorney is practicing law, but he doesn't need to practice on you. In Chapter 8 we'll discuss how to select an attorney to prepare your Living Trust and what it should cost you.

Let's see how well a will meets our estate planning objectives:

- <u>Choice of heirs</u>. This is the will at its best. It should do the job for you. At least you didn't let the government choose your heirs.

- <u>Probate</u>. A will means probate. You have guaranteed your family loss of time, loss of money, loss of control and loss of privacy.

- <u>Estate taxes</u>. A simple will does nothing to save you estate taxes. Most, but not all, attorneys will recommend a testamentary trust if you are married and your estate exceeds $600,000. We will discuss testamentary trusts in the next chapter. If you have a will and no testamentary trust and you are married and your estate exceeds $600,000, you will pay too much estate tax. There was a major change in the estate tax law in 1981. Every will, with or without a testamentary trust, written before September 11, 1981 needs to be reviewed and brought into conformity with the new law. As long as you need to renew your old will, if you have one, why not do yourself a favor and establish a Complete Estate Plan with a Living Trust instead?

- <u>Death income taxes</u>. The will does nothing to help here. Remember, your joint tenancy property supercedes your will. The surviving spouse will pay the maximum death income taxes unless the property is converted into community property. But if you do this in conjunction with a will instead of with a Living Trust, you've added another asset to your probate estate, which means more probate fees.

- <u>Conservatorship</u>. Wills take effect on your death. They have no effect dur-

ing your lifetime. Conservatorship is a problem of the living. The virtue of a <u>Living</u> Trust is that its just that — <u>Living</u>. It's designed for both life and death situations. A properly drawn Living Trust will avoid conservatorships. A will can't, by its very nature.

- <u>Control over assets</u>. Control stops upon incapacity or death of the first spouse. After then you're dealing with lawyers and judges (other names for loss of time, loss of money, loss of privacy and loss of control).

- <u>Flexibility</u>. During your lifetime, you can amend your will as often as you wish and can afford. If you do it often, however, you're inviting a court challenge from someone who was included earlier and excluded later. After either incapacity or the death of the first spouse, much flexibility is lost.

- <u>Privacy</u>. A will means loss of privacy. What should be a private family affair becomes the public's business. The government is being called in to govern the administration of your estate. The government's business, and now your business, is conducted in public with full public access to what should be your private family affairs.

Chapter 4

What's Wrong with a Will?

Advantages and Disadvantages of a Will Without a Testamentary Trust

Advantages

- Allows you to select your heirs.
- Allows you to select your executor.
- Allows you to waive a bond for your executor.
- Allows you to select a guardian for your minor or incapacitated children.

Disadvantages

- A will means probate.
- You cannot delay distribution to your heirs.
- Does nothing to minimize estate taxes.
- Does nothing to eliminate death income taxes.
- Does nothing to help if you become incapacitated.
- Gives you a false sense of security that you've properly planned your estate.

- <u>Health care</u>. A will takes effect on your death. It can't and won't deal with incapacitating illnesses and all the attendant problems. Only a Complete Estate Plan with a Living Trust will do this for you.

- <u>Funeral and burial instructions</u>. Most wills do a good job in setting forth funeral and burial instructions. The problem, when there is one, is that many people bury their wills. They're at a lawyer's office or in a safe deposit box and aren't located until after the funeral. The Complete Estate Plan gets your family involved in your estate plan at an earlier stage. Those who need to know will know exactly where to look to find your funeral and burial instructions.

- <u>Anatomical gifts</u>. This can be done in a will. We haven't seen it often, though. The problem with making an anatomical gift in your will is the same as for your funeral and burial instructions. By the time the will is located, it may be too late. Because the Complete Estate Plan is dynamic and invites activity rather than the passivity of a will, those who need to know should be able to find and implement your wishes in a timely manner.

- <u>Administration of estate</u>. You have made the administration of your estate as slow, expensive and difficult as the probate system will allow. We know you meant well when you signed your will, but did you really accomplish anything more than selecting your own heirs rather than letting the government do it for you?

Lawyers know it's hard to get most people to write a will. It takes time; it takes some thought; and it costs money. We will attempt to show you that for almost the same investment in time, thought and money, you can do yourself a real favor and establish a Complete Estate Plan with a Living Trust instead of a will. Please read on. We're only going to give you one more example of the wrong way to go before we start explaining the right way.

Chapter 5
What's Wrong with a Testamentary Trust?

First, let us describe what a trust is. This part of the discussion applies no matter what kind of a trust we'll be dealing with, whether it's a Living Trust, a testamentary trust, a revocable trust, an irrevocable trust, an Insurance Trust, etc., etc.

Trusts come to us from our English common law system and go back to at least medieval times, as far back as we have any reliable history of the English common law system. There are also records of the use of trusts in the ancient Roman law system. A trust breaks down the concept of ownership of property into three component parts: (1) control; (2) legal title; and (3) beneficial ownership. The true or original owner of property (the one who has legal control of the property) who wants to create a trust is usually called the trustor, although sometimes is also called the grantor or settlor. (The legal system delights in keeping things confusing. We'll try to keep things as simple as we can by consistently using the same words for the same ideas.) The holder of legal title (the person in whose name the property is held) is called the trustee. The person who gets the benefits from ownership of the property is called the beneficiary.

In order to create a trust, one or more trustors places property in the name of one or more trustees with written instructions on how to administer ownership of the property for the benefit of one or more beneficiaries.

The trustor, trustee and beneficiary may each be the same person or each may be different persons. The trustee and beneficiary may each have successors if the original person cannot or will not continue to act for any reason, such as death or incapacity. The trustor, trustee and beneficiary may each be individual persons or other entities, such as corporations or partnerships.

The government recognizes a trust as

Chapter 5

What's Wrong with a Testamentary Trust?

a sort of "artificial person," somewhat like a corporation. Most of us are more familiar with corporations than we are trusts, but trusts are just as well recognized in the law as are corporations. In a corporation people also place property in the hands of others to manage it for their benefit. In a sense shareholders are somewhat like trustors and beneficiaries and corporate directors are somewhat like trustees.

Both corporations and trusts are recognized by the government as having an independent existence apart from the existence of the people or property involved. Corporations may exist perpetually, but trusts may not. You may ask why this might be so. The answer is historical rather than the result of any modern policy decision. All law students spend days, even weeks, studying the ancient Rule Against Perpetuities. You don't need to worry about this. All you need to worry about in establishing a trust is finding an attorney who is experienced in setting up trusts and he or she will take care of all legal technicalities, including the Rule Against Perpetuities. If your lawyer starts to explain the Rule Against Perpetuities to you, change the subject to something more interesting, which would be just about anything else.

People frequently refer to the actual written document establishing the trust as the trust itself. Technically this is incorrect. The written document is really properly referred to as a "declaration of trust." The trust itself is intangible. It is a legal concept, just as the corporation is a legal concept. The trust encompasses all of its parts, the trustor, the trustee, the beneficiaries, the property in the trust, the written documents creating the trust and any amendments. But for practical purposes, you can think of a trust as a basket into which you put your property.

Testamentary trusts are trusts that become effective on the death of the trustor. They have no effect whatsoever during the lifetime of the trustor. The terms of a testamentary trust are usually set forth in a will, but sometimes are set forth in a separate document which gets incorporated into the will.

There are three primary uses for a testamentary trusts: (1) control of estate distribution beyond the first beneficiary; (2) delay of the ultimate distribution of the estate; and (3) minimization or elimination of estate taxes.

An example of the first use is the most typical one. A spouse with children from a prior marriage wants to leave everything to the second spouse but wants to make sure that the second spouse doesn't disinherit his or her children from the first marriage. Instead of passing the property directly to the second spouse, who could waste it or who could disinherit the stepchildren, it passes instead to a trust for the benefit of the second spouse during his or her lifetime and then at the death of the second spouse it goes to the children of the first marriage.

The second primary use of a testamentary trust is to delay the ultimate distribution of the estate. Parents are frequently concerned that their beneficiaries, usually their children or grandchildren, will not be mature enough to handle an immediate outright distribution of the entire estate. Instead of giving the property directly to the beneficiaries, it goes to a trust which usually provides that the income from the property will be used for the education, support and maintenance of the beneficiaries, but delays distribution of the principal until a later date, usually when the beneficiary reaches a specified age such as 25 or 30. Often there is a tiered distribution, such as one-third at 25, one-third at 30 and one-third at 35. This allows an immature beneficiary to lose only a limited amount on parties and trips to Europe and, hopefully, to learn a lesson before full distribution is made. In some cases, little or no distribution of principal is actually made during the beneficiary's lifetime, giving him or her

only income. (If the trust is going to continue beyond the lifetime of everyone named in the trust, your lawyer does have to begin worrying about compliance with the Rule Against Perpetuities.)

Delayed distribution trusts usually contain what is called a "spendthrift" clause. This means that the creditors of the beneficiary can only reach property when it comes out of the trust and never when it is in the trust. Also, with a spendthrift clause, the beneficiary will not be able to pledge his or her interest in the trust to secure loans. In most cases this means that creditors will only be able to attach income or principal when actually distributed out of the trust.

The third principal use of testamentary trusts is to eliminate or minimize estate taxes. This is useful only for married couples. Single people receive a federal estate tax exemption of $600,000. Married people receive the same exemption, but unless they properly plan their estate, the second $600,000 exemption will be lost. It's the government's way of saying "Gotchya!"

The device used to minimize estate taxes is the A-B Trust that we mentioned in Chapter One. It is important to understand that the A-B Trust is a device that can be used in either a testamentary trust or in a Living Trust. An

What's Wrong with a Testamentary Trust?

A-B Trust is a type of testamentary trust. It is also a type of Living Trust. The A-B Trust either goes into effect during the lifetime of the trustor (the Living Trust) or on the death of the trustor (the testamentary trust). In the next chapter we will show you why the Living Trust is a superior A-B Trust to the testamentary trust version of the A-B Trust. However, if properly done, the A-B Trust will minimize or eliminate estate taxes for married persons equally well in either a Living Trust or in a testamentary trust.

The A-B Trust (or in some cases the A-B-C Trust) should be used whenever the net estate of the married couple (including life insurance death benefits) is anticipated to exceed $600,000 at the death of the second to die. The A-B Trust divides the estate in two: the A trust which is the surviving spouse's revocable trust and the B Trust which is the deceased spouse's irrevocable trust (which should be limited to $600,000). Only the B Trust is taxed at the death of the first to die. Since the amount in the B Trust will not exceed $600,000, there will never be an estate tax on the B Trust. The A Trust is only taxed at the death of the surviving spouse, at which time it will receive its own $600,000 exemption. Using the A-B Trust properly, the married couple will pass up to $1,200,000 free of estate taxes rather than just $600,000.

The A-B-C Trust may also be incorporated into a testamentary trust or a Living Trust. As you remember (you are remembering this stuff, aren't you?), the A-B-C Trust is used for married couples whose net estate is anticipated to exceed $1,200,000 on the date of the death of the first spouse to die and one or both spouses wants to make certain that he or she controls the distribution of his or her full one-half of the estate after the death of the second to die.

Assume an estate of $2,000,000. On the death of the first to die, $1,000,000 goes in the A Trust, $600,000 in the B Trust and $400,000 in the C Trust. The A Trust is revocable and the beneficiaries of the A Trust may be changed by the survivor. Both the B and the C Trust become irrevocable after the death of the first to die and the survivor may not change the beneficiaries of the B Trust or the C Trust. $600,000 in the B Trust is taxed at the death of the first spouse, but since it's fully exempt, no tax is paid. Since the C Trust is a Q-TIP trust, it is also exempt from tax on the death of the first spouse. The A Trust in excess of $600,000 at the death of the second spouse to die and the full amount in the C Trust will be taxed when the second spouse dies. Just as with the A-B Trust,

What's Wrong with a Testamentary Trust?

**Comparison of Division of a $2,000,000 Estate with an A-B Trust
and an A-B-C Trust**

A-B Trust

A Trust $1,400,000	B Trust $600,000

A-B-C Trust

A Trust $1,000,000	B Trust $600,000	C Trust $400,000

Chapter 5

What's Wrong with a Testamentary Trust?

$1,200,000 was exempt from taxation, but unlike the A-B Trust, the first spouse to die controlled ultimate distribution of one-half of the estate ($1,000,000 in our example) instead of just $600,000.

Most attorneys who plan estates use a fairly simple formula: (1) most single people get a will with no trust (unless for some reason they want to delay distribution of their estate, in which case they get a testamentary A Trust); (2) most married couples who anticipate that their net estate will be less than $600,000 at the death of the second spouse to die get two wills with no trusts (again, unless they want to delay distribution of their estate, in which case they get testamentary A Trusts); (3) most married people whose net estate is anticipated to be between $600,000 and $1,200,000 get wills with testamentary A-B Trusts; (4) most married people whose net estate is anticipated to exceed $1,200,000 get wills with testamentary A-B Trusts unless there is concern over equal control of ultimate distribution, in which case they get wills with testamentary A-B-C Trusts.

Have these attorneys done a service for their clients? Yes and no. They've done an excellent job of minimizing or eliminating estate taxes where they could, but they've completely failed to eliminate probate. The will means pro-

bate, with all of its loss of time, loss of money, loss of control and loss of privacy.

The estate planning attorney who prepares a will with a testamentary trust has only done part of the job for you, but he or she has done a complete job for his or her law firm. He or she will be able to charge you right now for the full estate planning job of preparing the wills and testamentary trusts and he or she will be able to charge you twice again for each probate later on down the road. No matter what law firm you hire to do your probate, you always seem to end up with Dilley, Dally, Doolittle & Stahl. (We didn't make up that name. Credit belongs to Phil Frank, a San Francisco Chronicle cartoonist.)

Let's take a look at how well the testamentary trust meets our estate planning objectives.

- Choice of heirs. The will that comes with your testamentary trust should do an excellent job for you.

- Probate. The testamentary trust totally fails here. It puts you through the unnecessary and undesirable extra step of probate before your assets go into the trust. As you will see in the next chapter, the Living Trust allows you to place your assets in the

60

trust while you are still alive, skipping the probate process entirely. A real tragedy is that people who go to the time, trouble and expense of seeing an attorney to plan their estate are deluded into believing that they've done everything possible to protect their families. It's bad enough when those of us who don't plan are penalized, but it's tragic when those of us who do plan are still penalized.

- Estate taxes. A properly prepared testamentary trust will do an excellent job of minimizing or eliminating estate taxes, but remember, it won't do any better of a job than a Living Trust, which will also eliminate probate.

- Death income taxes. The testamentary trust doesn't work well on eliminating death income taxes. You have two choices (both bad): you can either keep your property in joint tenancy to eliminate probate and expose yourself to death income taxes or you can convert your property to community property to avoid the death income taxes, but then expose your property to probate. By eliminating the possibility of probate, the Living Trust completely solves this problem. By putting your property in the Living Trust and con-

verting it to community property, you eliminate probate and the death income tax at the same time.

- Conservatorship. Wills and testamentary trusts are both documents that only take effect upon your death. They make no attempt at all to solve problems during your lifetime. By their very nature, they cannot. If you're concerned about conservatorship, and we all should be, the Complete Estate Plan with a Living Trust is the only estate plan which deals with incapacity and conservatorship and allows you to avoid this embarrassing, cumbersome and expensive process.

- Control over assets. A will with a testamentary trust does an excellent job, but no better of a job than a Living Trust.

- Flexibility. During your lifetime you can amend your will and testamentary trust as many times as you choose, but each change requires a trip to your lawyer's office.

- Privacy. Not only will your assets and will be a public record, but all of the terms of your testamentary trust will also be public. This is completely unnecessary with a Living Trust. The

Chapter 5

What's Wrong with a Testamentary Trust?

Advantages and Disadvantages of a Will With a Testamentary Trust

Advantages

- Allows you to select your heirs.
- Allows you to delay distribution to your heirs.
- Allows you to select your executor.
- Allows you to waive a bond for your executor.
- Allows you to select a guardian for your minor or incapacitated children.
- Allows you to minimize estate taxes.

Disadvantages

- A will means probate, even with a testamentary trust.
- Does nothing to eliminate death income taxes.
- Does nothing to help if you become incapacitated.
- Gives you a false sense of security that you've properly planned your estate.

What's Wrong with a Testamentary Trust?

real shame is that if you have a testamentary trust you have gone to the time, trouble, and expense of planning your estate and you still haven't achieved something as simple and fundamental as privacy.

• Health care. Again, this is a problem that has to be attended to before death and your will and testamentary trust can't help you here, even if they wanted to.

• Funeral and burial instructions. Most wills, with or without testamentary trusts, cover this well. The major problem, as we've stated previously, is that often the will isn't found or read until after the funeral and burial. The Complete Estate Plan with a Living Trust helps by making the estate planning process an active one for those of you who choose to be involved, and gets all of your estate planning materials, including funeral and burial instructions, organized in a place and manner that's most likely to be consulted prior to the funeral.

• Anatomical gifts. The testamentary trust doesn't really add anything to your ability to get this done effectively.

• Administration of estate. You thought you did your job. You thought through who you wanted to be your heirs. You figured out the value of your net estate. You consulted and paid for an attorney. You signed a thick, multi-paged document that looked like it planned every aspect of your estate. And after all of this, you have still made the administration of your estate as slow, expensive and difficult as the probate system will allow. That's the answer to the question posed by the title of this chapter. That's what's wrong with a testamentary trust.

You can accomplish everything and anything you can accomplish with a testamentary trust with a Living Trust, but with a Living Trust you can also avoid probate, avoid death income taxes and create a Complete Estate Plan which deals with the lifetime problems of conservatorship avoidance and health care decisions.

Our next chapter deals with exactly how the Living Trust accomplishes your major estate planning goals.

Chapter 6
Can a Living Trust Solve My Problems?

As you might have guessed by now, the answer to the question posed by this chapter title is simple — YES. What we intend to do in this chapter is to describe exactly how the Living Trust works and how it solves each major estate planning goal. In the next chapter we will discuss the other elements of a Complete Estate Plan.

All trusts, no matter what their function, are either living trusts (taking effect during your lifetime) or testamentary trusts (taking effect only after you die). All trusts, no matter what their function, are either revocable (can be modified or even eliminated) or irrevocable (cannot be modified or eliminated).

What we, and most estate planners, call the Living Trust (with a capital "L" and a capital "T") is a revocable living trust — a trust that goes into effect during your lifetime that can be modified or even eliminated at any time during your lifetime.

There are other names for the Living Trust. For example, the inter vivos trust (lawyers like Latin — it keeps things confusing) or the grantor trust. We like to keep things simple and use the same name for the same thing whenever possible. However, you should be aware that your friends at the IRS use the term "grantor trust" instead of Living Trust. If you are ever unfortunate enough to be speaking or writing to the IRS, it's probably best to use the term "grantor trust" when referring to your Living Trust. Bureaucracies tend to get confused if you don't do things their way.

Don't be concerned, however, in dealing with the IRS. The Living Trust is a well known device to the IRS and there is no prejudice against it. The IRS clearly recognizes the A-B Trust and the A-B-C Trust whether they're found in testamentary trusts or in Living Trusts. There are specific provisions in the tax laws dealing with A-B Trusts and A-B-

Chapter 6

Can a Living Trust Solve My Problems?

Types of Trusts

Revocable

Can be changed, modified, amended or revoked by trustors.

Irrevocable

Cannot be changed, modified, amended or revoked by trustors.

Inter vivos

Becomes effective during the lifetime of the trustors.

Testamentary

Becomes effective at the death of the trustors.

The Living Trust is a revocable inter vivos trust. If a Living Trust has A Trust provisions, it will remain revocable at any time during the lifetime of a single trustor or during the lifetimes of both married trustors. If a Living Trust has A-B Trust or A-B-C Trust provisions, the entire Living Trust is revocable while both spouses are alive; however, after the death of the first spouse, the B Trust and (if there is one) the C Trust become irrevocable. The A Trust remains revocable during the lifetime of the surviving spouse.

Can a Living Trust Solve My Problems?

C Trusts. The IRS views the Living Trust primarily as a device to avoid probate, and the IRS could care less whether or not you pay probate fees because probate fees don't get paid to the IRS.

There are many forms that the Living Trust can take, but they all have a common structure. Every trust must have a trustor, a trustee and a beneficiary. If you have been running your own affairs in the past, there is no reason why you shouldn't continue to fill all three roles yourself.

As trustor, you transfer your property to yourself, as trustee, for your own benefit, as beneficiary. If that sounds a little bit like legal magic, you're right to some extent. You've gone through a legal formality that the law recognizes. You've created a trust, a separate legal entity, because you've taken the steps that the law requires to create that entity. It's a little bit like incorporating your business. It's still the same old business, but you file certain documents with the government, start calling your business a corporation, start calling yourself the president instead of the owner and complying with other formalities. Do all this, and the government recognizes you as a corporation.

Fortunately, there's much less formality in creating a trust than there is in forming a corporation. In order to create the trust you do need a legal document, a declaration of trust. But, unlike the document you need to form a corporation, you do not need to file it with any government agency. It's a completely private document.

Why go to the trouble of creating a separate legal entity? Simply because whatever property you transfer to the trust is no longer owned by you. Instead, it's owned by the trust, which is a separate legal entity from you. The trust, like a corporation, will continue to exist after you die. It will be run by your co-trustee or successor trustee after your death. Only property you own at the date of your death can be probated. If you've transferred all of your assets to the trust prior to your death, you will own no assets to probate at your death.

We know many of you are concerned that if you transfer your assets to a trust you might lose some control or flexibility in dealing with them. Nothing could be further from the truth. Since you will either be the sole trustee or co-trustee with your spouse, the property will still be in your own name (with a few extra words added to show you own it as trustee); you retain complete control and flexibility. A properly written Living Trust gives the trustee every con-

Chapter 6

Can a Living Trust Solve My Problems?

ceivable power to deal with trust assets. There is absolutely no loss of control or flexibility at any time during the joint lifetimes of the trustors. Moreover, since the Living Trust is revocable, it can always be modified or eliminated at any time during the joint lifetimes of the trustors. If there are co-trustors, as is usually the case with married couples, it takes both trustors to modify the Living Trust, but either trustor may revoke it.

There are no adverse tax effects caused by establishing a Living Trust. You continue to file state and federal income tax returns exactly as you did before you created your Living Trust. Since the trust is revocable, the IRS treats it as though it doesn't exist. You continue to file both state and federal tax returns under your own social security number. No separate tax I.D. number is required during your lifetime. When you die and the entire trust (in the case of an A Trust) or a part of the trust (the B Trust in an A-B Trust or the B and C Trusts in the case of an A-B-C Trust) becomes irrevocable, then and only then are separate tax returns and tax I.D. numbers required.

In California, property taxes are not affected by a transfer of your real property from you to your Living Trust. Because of Proposition 13 and appreciating real estate prices in California, it is vital that any transfer not trigger a reassessment. Fortunately, shortly after Proposition 13 was passed by the voters, the legislature specifically exempted transfers to Living Trusts from reassessment. This is also true in most states that followed California's lead by passing property tax laws similar to Proposition 13. When your property is deeded from you to your Living Trust, you will be supplied with a form to complete which attests to the fact that the transfer was to a Living Trust and, therefore, exempt from reassessment. As you will see later, we recommend that the attorney who prepares your Living Trust handle real estate transfers to the Living Trust. He or she should also complete this form for you.

Most real estate transfers require a transfer tax. Again, however, transfers to your Living Trust are specifically exempt. Both the deed transferring the real property to the Living Trust and the document exempting the transfer from reassessment under Proposition 13 contain the appropriate warranties exempting the transfer from transfer taxes. Again, the attorney who prepares your Living Trust should take care of this for you.

Transfers of assets other than real estate to the Living Trust are simple, and you can do them yourself with some in-

Can a Living Trust Solve My Problems?

There Are No Adverse Tax Consequences When You Establish a Living Trust

- Federal and state income tax returns are unchanged until death of first spouse.

- There is no reassessment of real property tranferred to the Living Trust.

- There are no transfer taxes for real property transferred to the Living Trust.

- There are no gift taxes resulting from forming or funding a Living Trust.

- The basis of property transferred to the Living Trust remains unchanged.

Chapter 6

Can a Living Trust Solve My Problems?

structions from your attorney. Assets are transferred to your name, as trustee, with reference to the date of the declaration of trust. Assume John Doe and Mary Doe signed their Living Trust on March 1, 1990. In order to put assets into the Living Trust, they would change the title to read "John Doe and Mary Doe, Trustees, U.D.T., dated March 1, 1990." The "U.D.T." means "under declaration of trust."

We recommend that you put virtually all your assets into the Living Trust as soon as possible. There are a few minor exceptions: (1) a small checking account; (2) motor vehicles; and (3) retirement plans.

Your usual checking account should be left out of the trust for convenience. Many people you have to deal with on a daily basis may think there is something special about a trust checking account and cause you some difficulty in cashing your checks. They would be wrong, of course, but you still don't need the trouble of having to explain the virtues of a Living Trust each time you want to cash a check at the supermarket. Just make sure you don't keep large amounts (anything that would cause the gross value of your assets outside the Living Trust to exceed $60,000) in your checking account. For most of us, that's not usually a problem; however, if you sell

an asset with substantial value, such as your home, make certain that you park your funds in your savings account or a money market fund inside the Living Trust and not in your checking account.

Motor vehicles are normally kept out of Living Trusts because of the bureaucratic problems at the Department of Motor Vehicles. The DMV has its own way of doing everything. We recommend joint tenancy for vehicles owned by married couples. Remember, joint tenancy causes unnecessary death income taxes on appreciating property. Most motor vehicles, however, depreciate and won't cause you any tax problems. If you do happen to own either extremely valuable vehicles (enough to get the value of your gross estate outside your Living Trust to exceed $60,000) or the rare vehicle that would significantly appreciate in value (such as some antique vehicles), it may be worth your trouble to deal with the Department of Motor Vehicles.

Because most unmarried people have successor trustees and not co-trustees, they may want to consider having their checking accounts and motor vehicles inside their Living Trust, despite the inconvenience. This will insure that there's no chance of a probate for these assets.

The last type of asset to keep out of

Can a Living Trust Solve My Problems?

Advantages and Disadvantages of Naming Your Living Trust as the Beneficiary of Your Retirement Benefits such as IRAs, Pension Plans, Keogh Plans, 401(k) Plans

Advantages

- The funds will be distributed in accordance with the terms of the Living Trust.

- Distribution to children can be delayed.

Disadvantages

- If an entity, such as a Living Trust, is the beneficiary, all proceeds must be paid out in a lump sum. If an individual, such as a spouse or adult child, is the beneficiary, the proceeds may be paid over a period of years, allowing the beneficiary to spread and possibly reduce income taxes.

Can a Living Trust Solve My Problems?

your Living Trust is retirement benefits such as IRAs, 401(k) plans, pension plans and profit sharing plans. You should never change the <u>ownership</u> of pensions, profit sharing plans, IRAs or 401(k) plans to your Living Trust. You could change the <u>beneficiary</u> of these plans to your Living Trust, but we recommend, instead, that you designate your spouse to be the primary beneficiary and your Living Trust to be the contingent beneficiary. These benefits pass directly to the beneficiary without having to go through probate.

All other assets of value, including the death benefits of your life insurance policies, should be placed in the name of the Living Trust. This includes real estate, stocks, bonds, your business, partnerships, household goods, personal property, etc. Transfer of all of these assets is simple except for real estate. The attorney who prepares your Living Trust can transfer your real property and show you how to transfer all other assets. If you happen to be in the real estate business, you may even be able to transfer your own real estate. Others should not attempt this on their own.

If you leave assets out of your Living Trust and their gross value exceeds $60,000, they will be subject to probate and you will not have achieved the full value of your Living Trust.

When you acquire new assets there is no need to amend your Living Trust. Just acquire them in the name of the Living Trust rather than your own name. If you forget to do so (please don't), you can always transfer them to the Living Trust at a later date.

The Living Trust is totally flexible. You live your life the way you always have. You pay no more and no less income taxes during your lifetime than you would have without a Living Trust. Just remember to keep all assets (other than a small checking account, motor vehicles and retirement plans) inside the protective walls of your Living Trust.

We recommend that you make a quick review of your Complete Estate Plan and Living Trust once a year to make certain that: (1) your estimate of your gross estate is still accurate; (2) your desires for the distribution of your estate on your death are the same; (3) you haven't forgotten to put newly acquired assets into the Living Trust; and (4) your Durable Power of Attorney for Health Care and Directive to Physicians have not expired.

The means by which the transfer of assets takes place after death is simple with a Living Trust. If you are married, your spouse is probably co-trustee of your Living Trust. Title is already in his or her name as co-trustee. All the surviving spouse need do is remove the deceased spouse from the title by sending the appropriate parties a death certificate and a simple letter of instructions. If real estate is involved, an Affidavit of Death must be filed which, if prepared by our office, will cost about $125. On the death of an unmarried person, including the surviving spouse, a successor trustee, named in the trust, distributes the assets in accordance with the terms of the Living Trust. This should take a matter of days, rather than months or years as in probate, and should involve minimal transfer fees and postage costs rather than the thousands of dollars in probate fees and costs. Our office provides its clients and their successor trustees with a simple letter of instruction on the death of any trustor of one of our Living Trusts. Take a look at Appendix K in the back of the book for a checklist of what to do when someone dies.

In addition to eliminating the probate process, the Living Trust also eliminates the need for conservatorship proceedings of your assets. Since you don't own anything as an individual once you've transferred all your assets to the Living Trust, the conservatorship laws are not applicable to your property. Instead, the terms of the Living Trust control. In the case of incapacity, as defined in the Living Trust, your co-trustee spouse (or

successor trustee if you are unmarried) takes control of management of the Living Trust, privately and without the cost and humiliation of a public proceeding. A well written Living Trust makes specific provisions for incapacity.

As you are reading this, it's becoming obvious that you must select your co-trustee and successor trustee with great care. The name says it all. Select a trustee whom you can trust. (The law imposes severe restrictions on self-dealing by trustees, but no one wants to be involved with a lawsuit.) Most of us will choose our spouse as co-trustee and one or more of our adult children as successor trustee. If you have more than one adult child, you can, if you choose, make them joint successor trustees with majority rule. This is extremely flexible. You can do almost anything you want. The key is to do what makes you comfortable. With a Living Trust, you get to make these decisions instead of the government.

If after establishing your Living Trust you find yourself in the unfortunate position of no longer trusting your spouse, you can always unilaterally terminate the Living Trust. In a divorce situation, we usually recommend that the family Living Trust be terminated and that each party set up his or her own separate Living Trust with the assets each re-

Can a Living Trust Solve My Problems?

ceived out of the divorce. The Living Trust will not help you during a divorce, but fortunately it will not hinder you in any way either.

If you believe your children are not capable of acting as successor trustees, you have to consider other alternatives, such as friends, other relatives, professional or financial advisors or trust departments of financial institutions. Normally we encourage you to use professionals only for advice and not as your successor trustees. Your successor trustee can always hire these people for their advice when needed. An important factor in choosing your successor trustee is whether or not your Living Trust provides for delayed distribution. If there is to be no delay in distribution, the successor trustee's duties are fairly simple. He or she only needs to distribute the assets in accordance with the terms of the Living Trust document. However, if there is to be a delay in distribution after the death of the second spouse, the successor trustee must manage the assets until final distribution — a much greater responsibility.

The Living Trust avoids probate and avoids conservatorship equally well for both single people and married couples. Once your gross estate begins to exceed $60,000, all people, whether or not they have any tax problems, should begin to consider the Living Trust. By the time your gross estate reaches $100,000 it is clear that you should have a Living Trust. Probate fees are over $6,000 on a $100,000 gross estate. Remember also, inflation is making your estate grow every day whether you do anything to help it along, and liabilities are not deducted to determine the amount of your gross estate.

Married couples, however, can save even more by minimizing or even eliminating estate taxes and death income taxes. Unfortunately these tax planning opportunities are not available to single people through the Living Trust. Single people can still use gifting programs or establish other tax saving trusts, however. More on that later.

As we explained earlier, many married couples have unnecessarily exposed themselves to death income taxes by putting some or all of their assets in joint tenancy to avoid probate. Their desire to avoid probate was commendable, but in most cases they have ignored the fact that they only avoided the first probate. When the second spouse dies, the entire estate will usually be probated. But even if the surviving spouse attempts to solve this by forming new joint tenancies (with all the problems of having a non-spouse as a joint tenant) or by entering into a Living Trust (better late than never), the couple still has unnecessarily exposed themselves to death income taxes.

With a joint tenancy only one-half of the value of the asset gets stepped-up in basis on the death of the first spouse. If the same property were held as community property, 100% of the value of the asset would get stepped-up in basis on the death of the first spouse. The Living Trust allows you to own any property in the Living Trust as either community property or as separate property. It doesn't lose that characteristic because it's in the Living Trust.

Once your Living Trust is formed, it is absolutely essential to put all property held in joint tenancy with your spouse (except for most motor vehicles and small checking accounts) into the Living Trust and convert it to community property. The Living Trust is the only estate planning vehicle that allows you to both avoid probate and eliminate death income taxes on the same property.

If after your spouse's death you find yourself wanting to sell any asset that has appreciated, such as your home, you will thank yourself many times over for your good sense in having a Living Trust. (If we've helped you come to that decision in this book, we will also gladly accept thank-you notes.)

In addition to avoiding probate for all people, in addition to avoiding conserva-torship for all people and in addition to eliminating death income taxes for married people holding appreciated property in joint tenancy, the Living Trust will minimize or eliminate the estate tax for married couples whose gross estate will exceed $600,000 on the death of the second spouse to die.

As we have shown you earlier, the A-B Trust and the A-B-C Trust can be in either a testamentary trust or in a Living Trust, with the difference being that the testamentary trust forces you into the agony of probate and the Living Trust does not. As a means to avoid estate taxes the Living Trust works just as well as the best testamentary trust, with a lot of extra benefits and none of the disadvantages of the testamentary trust that we've mentioned.

Remember, estate tax avoidance "maxes out" after your estate reaches $1,200,000, unless insurance proceeds bring it over that amount. In that case we recommend an Insurance Trust — an entirely separate trust from your Living Trust. Also, if your estate is likely to exceed $1,200,000 you should consider using the $10,000 annual gift tax exemption or other trusts we'll mention later to reduce your taxable estate.

Let's take a look at three couples each with an estate of $1,200,000 for a moment. To make our example simple, we'll

Chapter 6

Can a Living Trust Solve My Problems?

Couple X (simple will)

Gross estate	$1,200,000
Probate fees on husband's death	-26,300
Net estate	1,173,700
Estate taxes on husband's death	-0-
Distribution to wife	1,173,700
Probate fees on wife's death	-45,774
Taxable estate	1,127,926
Estate taxes on wife's death	-205,450
Disribution to children	$ 922,476

Couple Y (will and testamentary trust)

Gross estate	$1,200,000
Probate fees on husband's death	-26,300
Net estate	1,173,700
Estate taxes on husband's death	-0-
Distribution to wife	1,173,700
Probate fees on wife's death	-45,774
Taxable estate	1,127,926
Estate taxes on wife's death	-0-
Distribution to children	$1,127,926

Couple Z (with a Living Trust)

Gross estate	$1,200,000
Probate fees on husband's death	-0-
Net estate	1,200,000
Estate taxes on husband's death	-0-
Distribution to wife	1,200,000
Probate fees on wife's death	-0-
Taxable estate	1,200,000
Estate taxes on wife's death	-0-
Distribution to children	$1,200,000

assume no liabilities, so the net estate and the gross estate are both $1,200,000. Assume Couple X have a will without a testamentary trust. Couple Y have a will with a testamentary A-B Trust. Couple Z have an A-B Living Trust.

We'll assume, that like most couples, the distribution is to be all to the surviving spouse on the death of the first spouse to die and then all to the children in equal shares on the death of the second spouse to die. For convenience, we'll assume the husband dies first. We'll also assume (fairly unrealistically) that the only probate costs are the statutory fees. For convenience, we'll forget about extraordinary fees, appraiser's fees, etc., etc.

When Husband X dies with only a will, his probate estate is $600,000. Probate fees will be $26,300. There will be no estate tax. When Wife X dies, her probate estate will be $1,173,700, which is the $600,000 she received from her husband less his probate fees of $26,300 plus her own $600,000. Her probate fees will be $45,774. Estate taxes will be charged on $1,127,926, which is the balance of her estate less probate fees, for a total estate tax of $205,450. Probate fees on both estates and estate taxes on the wife's death have reduced the estate from $1,200,000 to $922,476.

When Husband Y dies with a will and a testamentary A-B Trust, his probate estate is $600,000. Probate fees will be $26,300. There will be no estate tax. When Wife Y dies, her probate estate will be $1,173,700, which is the $600,000 she received from her husband less his probate fees of $26,300 plus her own $600,000. Her probate fees will be $45,774. There will be no estate taxes. Probate fees on both estates have reduced the estate from $1,200,000 to $1,127,926.

When Husband Z dies with a Living Trust, there is no probate and no probate fees. There will be no estate tax. When Wife Z dies, she has the full $600,000 from her husband's estate plus her own $600,000. There will be no probate and no probate fees. There will be no estate taxes. The entire estate of $1,200,000 will pass to the children of Couple Z, undiminished by either probate fees or estate taxes.

Couple Z have saved $277,524 more than Couple X and $72,074 more than Couple Y by using their Living Trust.

For more examples of how much a Living Trust may save you, see Appendix F (single persons) or Appendix G (married couples).

In the examples we've given you so far in this book, it's been assumed that all couples with estates over $600,000 would use either an A-B Trust or an A-

Can a Living Trust Solve My Problems?

B-C Trust; however, there are two good reasons for couples with estates under $600,000 to at least consider using an A-B Trust: (1) the irrevocability of the B Trust on the death of the first spouse; and (2) potential growth of the estate.

The first reason relates to concern on the part of one or both spouses that the other might change the beneficiaries of his or her estate after the first spouse dies. Most often this involves the concern that children of a prior marriage will not continue to be provided for by the step-parent. But there can also be a concern that the surviving spouse will remarry and leave everything to the new spouse instead of the children. If there is any concern at all, then the A-B Trust works well for estates below $600,000 as well. This is because the B Trust becomes irrevocable on the death of the first spouse. While the survivor can use the assets of the B Trust to live on, he or she must leave whatever is left of those assets after his or her death to those designated by the first to die.

The second reason you might want to consider an A-B Trust even though your estate is now less than $600,000 is the possible growth of your estate. Inflation does amazing things. Think back twenty years ago. Think about what kind of house you could buy for $100,000. Think about what kind of a house you can buy for $100,000 now. Take two statistics into account: (1) the surviving spouse lives another ten years after the death of the first spouse to die, on the average; and (2) at 7% inflation, your estate doubles in ten years. We know this sounds a little "statistically" pat, but your $600,000 estate could easily be worth $1,200,000 in ten years. The estate that was only worth $600,000 at the date of the death of the first to die, might be worth $1,200,000 by the time the second spouse dies. Remember, it's the value at the date of the death of the second spouse to die that's important for this purpose.

While it may sound like the A-B Trust should be used by all married couples, there is one down-side feature you should take into account. After the death of the first spouse, the estate will be divided in two and thereafter two separate sets of tax records must be kept and two separate income tax returns must be filed. The surviving spouse will continue to file a Form 1040 under his or her social security number. However, once the B Trust becomes irrevocable on the death of the first to die, the IRS now recognizes it as a separate legal entity and the B Trust must file annual income tax returns on Form 1041. This extra effort is clearly worth it to make a substantial savings on estate taxes if you

Can a Living Trust Solve My Problems?

Rights of Surviving Spouse With a Typical A-B Trust

A Trust

- Unlimited.

B Trust

- May not modify.

- May manage all assets.

- May use all of the income from the B Trust.

- May use any or all of the principal of the B Trust if the assets of the A Trust are not sufficient or are impractical to use to maintain the same standard of living, including health care.

- Some Living Trusts allow the surviving spouse to spend up to the greater of $5,000 or 5% of the principal of the B Trust each year (non-cumulative) for any reason, no matter how frivolous. We recommend against including this right in most situations.

Chapter 6

Can a Living Trust Solve My Problems?

know your estate will exceed $600,000. Whether or not it is worth it if your estate is currently below that figure is a matter of personal preference. You will still want a Living Trust as long as your gross estate is $100,000 or more, but you may only want to use an A Trust.

This disadvantage is also similar to the choice you have to make in using the A-B-C Trust if your estate exceeds $1,200,000. Remember, there's no advantage to the A-B-C Trust if you're willing to put more in the A Trust than in the B Trust. Tax advantages are maximized at $600,000 in the A Trust and $600,000 in the B Trust. The A-B-C Trust is used to equalize the two estates so that the first to die ensures that he or she will control ultimate distribution of one-half of the estate and not just $600,000. The disadvantages of an A-B-C Trust are that they're usually slightly more expensive to form at the outset and that three set of separate records must be kept after the first to die passes away. Also, the surviving spouse has less flexibility under the A-B-C Trust because he or she may not use the principal of either the B or the C Trust unless he or she has exhausted the assets in the A Trust.

It is clear that the tax savings of the A-B Trust are worth the extra effort to file two tax returns annually. Since there are no extra tax savings with an A-B-C Trust, it is again a matter of personal preference as to whether or not it's worth this extra cost and effort in order to ensure control of distribution of your estate in excess of $600,000.

Remember, the extra tax returns would also have been necessary if you had a testamentary trust. It's the price married couples have to pay to obtain the second $600,000 estate tax exemption.

Aside from the extra tax returns, there are only four disadvantages that we've experienced that are specific to the Living Trust.

First, when you refinance real estate many lending institutions will require that you take the property out of your Living Trust. They are concerned that your Living Trust document may not have appropriate language allowing the trustees the power to refinance. If you have a properly drafted declaration of trust the trustees will, of course, have the power to refinance. They will have the power to do anything the trustors could have done had there been no trust. However, many lending institutions have developed a blanket rule against refinancing property in Living Trusts. The simple solution is to take the property out of the Living Trust during the refinancing and to immediately put it back

Can a Living Trust Solve My Problems?

Advantages and Disadvantages of a Living Trust

Advantages

- Avoids probate.
- Avoids conservatorship.
- Eliminates or reduces estate taxes.
- Eliminates death income taxes.
- Maintains privacy.
- Allows you to delay distribution to your heirs.
- Allows you to control your assets after death of spouse.

Disadvantages

- Probate provides a short statute of limitations to cut off creditor claims.
- Must transfer assets to the Living Trust.
- Makes refinancing of real estate a little more cumbersome.
- Makes use of the $10,000 per donor per donee annual gift tax exclusion a little more cumbersome.

Can a Living Trust Solve My Problems?

Estate Planning Alternates

Planning Alternative	Avoids Probate on Death of First Spouse	Avoids Probate on Death of Second Spouse	Provides Maximum Estate Tax Savings
No Will	No	No	No
Simple Will	No	No	No
Testamentary Trust	No	No	Yes
Joint Tenancy	Yes	No	No
Living Trust	Yes	Yes	Yes

Planning Alternative	Provides Maximum Death Tax Savings	Avoids Conservatorship	Provides Privacy
No Will	No	No	No
Simple Will	No	No	No
Testamentary Trust	No	No	No
Joint Tenancy	No	No	No
Living Trust	Yes	Yes	Yes

Can a Living Trust Solve My Problems?

into the Living Trust after the refinancing is completed. This is not a subterfuge on the lender. Most lenders suggest it themselves, and most title companies that handle the paper work for the refinancing will do all of this for you. Just make sure that you get the property back into your Living Trust as soon as possible.

The second disadvantage, if it is one, is that probate cuts off creditor claims unless they're filed within four months after the executor publishes notice of death and distributes assets. This can be an advantage if you're in a business or profession where you're likely to be sued after your death. The biggest problem, of course, is that probate <u>invites</u> creditors and potential creditors to file claims. It's simple to file a claim in an estate. No attorney is necessary. All in all, it's cheaper and faster for the creditor than a lawsuit would have been. With a Living Trust, there is no invitation to file a claim or a lawsuit. Creditors need not even be notified of the death. If any creditor wants to file a suit, he or she must hire an attorney and proceed with a civil lawsuit, which is much more expensive and time consuming than filing a creditor's claim in probate court. However, with a Living Trust the applicable statute of limitations, which controls when claims are barred for lack of

timely filing, is exactly the same as if the defendant were still alive. We recommend that your Living Trust contain a "creditors clause" which allows the co-trustee or successor trustee to probate a portion of your assets at your death if it is desirable at the time.

The third disadvantage is that if you want to make a gift, subject to the $10,000 annual exclusion, of an asset in your Living Trust, you should transfer the asset back to your own name prior to making the gift. If the gift comes directly from the Living Trust, you will lose the exclusion if you die within three years of making the gift.

The final disadvantage of a Living Trust is that you have to <u>do</u> <u>something</u>. You have to take the initiative to create the Living Trust and then put your assets in the name of the Living Trust. It's always easier to do nothing and to keep putting off until tomorrow what doesn't absolutely have to be done today. It's not easy for any of us to think about estate planning. However, for some reason, you have at least been motivated enough to read this far, so we know you're interested. The good news, as we will show you in Chapter 8, is that it is neither difficult nor expensive to establish a Living Trust. But you still do have to act. The choice is yours. You either make your own estate plan or you

Chapter 6

Can a Living Trust Solve My Problems?

Which Living Trust Do You Need?

A Trust

- All unmarried people.

- Most married couples whose net estate is not expected to exceed $600,000 at the death of the second spouse to die.

A-B Trust

- Some married couples whose net estate is not expected to exceed $600,000 at the death of the second spouse to die.

- All married couples whose net estate is expected to be between $600,000 and $1,200,000 at the death of second spouse to die.

- Most married couples whose net estate is expected to be over $1,200,000 at the death of either the first spouse to die or the second spouse to die.

A-B-C Trust

- Some married couples whose net estate is expected to be over $1,200,000 on the death of the first spouse to die.

Can a Living Trust Solve My Problems?

Typical Living Trust for an Unmarried Person

- Trustor is the sole trustee and beneficiary.

- Successor trustee is a close friend or adult child.

- Successor beneficiaries are trustor's heirs.

- All assets held in the Living Trust.

- Always an A Trust, never an A-B Trust or an A-B-C Trust.

Chapter 6

Can a Living Trust Solve My Problems?

Typical Living Trust for a Married Couple

- Trustors are co-trustees and co-beneficiaries.

- Successor trustees are one or more adult children.

- Distribution is all to surviving spouse and on death of surviving spouse to children in equal shares.

- All assets are held in the Living Trust, except a small checking account and most motor vehicles are kept in joint tenancy.

- May be either an A Trust, an A-B Trust or an A-B-C Trust, but usually will be an A-B Trust.

Can a Living Trust Solve My Problems?

Typical A Trust for Married Couple with Estate of Less Than $600,000

Period 1 - Both Spouses Alive

> 1985 Hill Family Trust
> Jack & Jill Hill, Co-trustees
> $500,000

Period 2 - Death of First Spouse

> 1985 Hill Living Trust
> Jill Hill, Trustee
> $500,000

Period 3 - Death of Second Spouse

> Daughter,
> Joan Hill
> $250,000

> Son,
> Jim Hill
> $250,000

> Uncle Sam
> -0-

Can a Living Trust Solve My Problems?

**Typical A-B Trust for Married Couple with Estate of More Than
$600,000 but Less Than $1,200,000**

Period 1 - Both Spouses Alive

> 1985 Hill Living Trust
> Jack & Jill Hill, Co-trustees
> $1,000,000

Period 2 - Death of First Spouse

> Survivor's Trust
> (A Trust)
> Jill Hill, Trustee
> $500,000

> Decedent's Trust
> (B Trust)
> Jill Hill, Trustee
> $500,000

Period 3 - Death of Second Spouse

> Daughter,
> Joan Hill
> $500,000

> Uncle Sam
> -0-

> Son,
> Jim Hill
> $500,000

Can a Living Trust Solve My Problems?

Typical A-B Trust for Married Couple with Estate of More Than $1,200,000

Period 1 - Both Spouses Alive

> 1985 Hill Living Trust
> Jack & Jill Hill, Co-trustees
> $2,000,000

Period 2 - Death of First Spouse

> Survivor's Trust
> (A Trust)
> Jill Hill, Trustee
> $1,400,000

> Decedent's Trust
> (B Trust)
> Jill Hill, Trustee
> $600,000

Period 3 - Death of Second Spouse

> Daughter,
> Joan Hill
> $840,250

> Uncle Sam
> $319,500

> Son,
> Jim Hill
> $840,250

Chapter 6

Can a Living Trust Solve My Problems?

Typical A-B-C Trust for Married Couple with Estate of More Than $1,200,000

Period 1 - Both Spouses Alive

> 1985 Hill Living Trust
> Jack & Jill Hill, Co-trustees
> $2,000,000

Period 2 - Death of First Spouse

Survivor's Trust	Decedent's Trust	QTIP Trust
(A Trust)	(B Trust)	(C Trust)
Jill Hill, Trustee	Jill Hill, Trustee	Jill Hill, Trustee
$1,000,000	$600,000	$400,000

Period 3 - Death of Second Spouse

Daughter, Joan Hill $840,250	Uncle Sam $319,500	Son, Jim Hill $840,250

Can a Living Trust Solve My Problems?

Typical A-B Trust for Married Couple with Separate Property and Children by Prior Marriage

Period 1 - Both Spouses Alive

1985 Hill Living Trust Jack & Jill Hill, Co-trustees	
Jack's separate property	$200,000
Jill's separate property	100,000
Jack & Jill's community property	100,000
TOTAL	$400,000

Period 2 - Death of First Spouse

Survivor's Trust (A Trust) Jill Hill, Trustee		Decedent's Trust (B Trust) Jill Hill, Trustee	
Jill's separate property	$100,000	Jack's separate property	$200,000
50% of community property	50,000	50% of community property	50,000
TOTAL	$150,000	TOTAL	$250,000

Period 3 - Death of Second Spouse

Jill's Daughter, Joan Hill $150,000		Jack's Son, Jim Hill $250,000

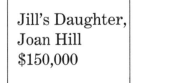

Uncle Sam
-0-

Chapter 6

Can a Living Trust Solve My Problems?

let the government do it for you.

In this chapter we've shown you how the Living Trust will accomplish most of your estate planning objectives: (1) avoid probate; (2) avoid conservatorship; (3) eliminate death income taxes; and (4) eliminate or minimize estate taxes. If you do nothing more for yourself than create a Living Trust, you will have done a better job of estate planning than 99% of the American public. But we recommend that you go one step further and create what we call a Complete Estate Plan. The Complete Estate Plan is centered around your Living Trust and is designed to give you and your family an estate plan that gives you ultimate protection in every life and death situation.

Chapter 7

What Do I Need for a Complete Estate Plan?

The concept of a Complete Estate Plan is to let you make legally enforceable decisions about the future now, while you're competent and alive. The Living Trust is the single best estate planning tool we've ever found, but it can only accomplish those things it was designed to accomplish: (1) avoid probate; (2) avoid conservatorship; (3) eliminate death income taxes; and (4) eliminate or minimize estate taxes. These are the major goals of good estate planning. The Complete Estate Plan is designed to both supplement and maximize the benefits you can obtain from your Living Trust.

Pour Over Will

After everything we've said about wills so far in this book, now we're going to tell you that you should have one. But not an ordinary will, a Pour Over Will. The difference between an ordinary will and a Pour Over Will is that an ordinary will is designed to get your assets into the probate system and the Pour Over Will is designed to act as an insurance policy. The Pour Over Will puts any asset you've forgotten to put into your Living Trust during your lifetime into the Living Trust at your death.

If you have done your job in getting your assets in the name of the Living Trust prior to your death, the Pour Over Will will have no effect at all, because it only governs assets outside the Living Trust. This is what we hope for. But, none of us is perfect. There are oversights. If you've neglected to put an asset into the Living Trust, it's still important that it get there, both for estate tax purposes and to allow you to chose who will get those assets.

If you're going to forget to put any property into your Living Trust, try to make certain that it's not worth more than $60,000. If you do so, the Pour Over Will will act just like any other will and get you into the probate court. For-

Chapter 7

What Do I Need for a Complete Estate Plan?

tunately, only the part of your estate that you've neglected to put into your Living Trust will be probated. The part that you have put into the Living Trust will still be safe from probate.

The lesson should be clear. If you're going to go to the effort of taking control of your life and death decisions by establishing a Complete Estate Plan with a Living Trust, <u>follow</u> <u>through</u>! Don't wait until next week or next month to start transferring your assets to the Living Trust. Don't acquire new assets in your own name instead of in the name of the Living Trust. Don't rob your family and yourself of the full benefits of your planning.

If you have minor children or an incapacitated adult child, your Pour Over Will should appoint a guardian or guardians of the child or children in case both you and your spouse die before they reach majority or remain incapacitated.

When choosing a guardian, many people want to name their brother or sister <u>and</u> <u>spouse</u> as co-guardians. This sounds good at the time, because we see our child placed in the care of a family and not just an individual. We recommend, however, that you name your blood relative as the sole guardian and not as co-guardian with your in-law. This is just to make certain that in case of a divorce, it is absolutely clear that you

want the care of your child to be with your sister and not with your brother-in-law (no matter how nice of a guy he may be). On the other hand, if you really do want your brother-in-law to be the guardian, say so. The beauty of estate planning is that you do get to make these decisions.

Assignment of Personal Property

We're sure that some of you have been concerned when we've urged you to put the title of all of your property into your Living Trust. That's easy for the kinds of property where there is formal title, such as real estate, stocks, bonds, businesses, partnerships, etc. But what about personal effects where there is no formal title, such as clothing, home furnishings, jewelry, silverware, etc.?

Again, the answer is simple. You sign a document — the Assignment of Personal Property — that formally transfers these assets to the Living Trust. Since there is no formal legal title, there is no need to register the transfer of title with anyone. The Assignment of Personal Property form is kept with your other Complete Estate Plan documents, and it alone is all that is legally necessary to evidence your intent to have these kinds of assets in your Living Trust.

What Do I Need for a Complete Estate Plan?

Letter of Instruction Regarding Personal Property

So far in this book we've been discussing distribution of your estate in terms of the bulk of it — what lawyers call the "residuary." But what about the ring you want to leave to your favorite niece or the clothing you want to give to your favorite charity?

We recommend that you leave these specific gifts outside of the terms of the Living Trust, so that you don't have to hire an attorney to amend the entire Living Trust document each time you decide to make a specific gift or change your mind about your niece, who just ran off to join a rock and roll band.

Instead, we recommend a separate Letter of Instruction Regarding Personal Property. Properly drafted, it is legally binding on your successor trustee, and you can easily amend it yourself, without an attorney.

Avoid the inevitable family friction of having each of your children saying "I know Dad would have wanted me to have his favorite pipe wrench!" You will ease the burden and trauma on your family if you make these decisions in advance.

Community Property Declaration

This is only for married couples. This is extraordinarily important if you have formerly held any of your property in joint tenancy with your spouse. This is the document that will give you the benefit of the full step-up in basis on appreciating property. It is the foundation of one of the most important benefits of proper estate planning.

If you or your spouse have any separate property — property that you had before you were married or that you were given or inherited and have not commingled with your community property — you might consider converting it to community property at this point by including it in your Community Property Declaration.

This should only be done with caution, however. Unlike property you've owned with your spouse in joint tenancy, your spouse has no legal rights to your separate property. If you are divorced, it's only the community property that's equally divided. You get to keep all of your separate property. On your death, you only control the disposition of one-half of your community property, but you control the disposition of all of your separate property.

Why would anyone convert their separate property to community? There are two good reasons. First, love and affection for your spouse, and second, to get the full step-up in basis when your spouse dies. If you hold an asset as your separate property when your spouse

What Do I Need for a Complete Estate Plan?

dies, you get <u>no</u> step-up in basis. It's worse than joint tenancy where you at least get a step-up in basis on one-half the value of the property.

You don't have to worry about gift taxes when you convert your separate property to community property because <u>all</u> gifts to spouses are exempt from gift taxes. Also, if the gift to a spouse is real estate, there is no reassessment under Proposition 13 and no transfer tax.

The process of converting separate property to community is easy and without immediate tax consequences, but the decision should be made with great care, because once made it can only be unmade with the consent of your spouse.

Durable General Power of Attorney

A power of attorney allows another person to act for you if you are not able or willing to act for yourself. A special power of attorney gives that person, called an "attorney-in-fact," the power to act in only specified situations. A general power of attorney gives your attorney-in-fact broad powers to act generally on your behalf.

The problem with most powers of attorney is that they're no longer valid just when they're most needed — incompetency. A special form of power of attorney can be created which survives incompetency. It's called a <u>durable</u> power

of attorney and it specifically allows another, usually your spouse or adult child, to act on your behalf in case you become incompetent.

The Durable General Power of Attorney that we recommend is another insurance policy, similar to the Pour Over Will. You should not need it, because if all of your assets are in the Living Trust, your co-trustee or successor trustee will use the incompetency clause to manage the Living Trust if you become mentally or physically unable to do so. However, if you've inadvertently left an asset out of the Living Trust and become incompetent, your attorney-in-fact just acts in your place and transfers the asset to the Living Trust on your behalf. Without the Durable General Power of Attorney, your family would be faced with a conservatorship proceeding just to transfer the asset to the Living Trust.

Durable Power of Attorney for Health Care

This durable power of attorney allows your attorney-in-fact to make medical decisions for you when you can't. We recommend that it should be a separate document from your Durable General Power of Attorney. There are special statutory requirements governing Durable Powers of Attorney for Health Care, including the requirement that it

What Do I Need for a Complete Estate Plan?

be renewed every seven years. Because of the special statutory rules governing only Durable Powers of Attorney for Health Care, we believe it to be unwise to combine it with any other document.

Both the Durable General Power of Attorney and the Durable Power of Attorney for Health Care take effect only when you become incompetent. They have no effect while you are competent, but they must be executed while you are still competent. Once you lose competency, it's too late. Your family is left no alternative but conservatorship proceedings.

Depending upon your specific wishes, Durable Powers of Attorney for Health Care can contain "right to die" provisions. Many, if not most, of us do not want to be kept alive artificially for extended periods when there is no hope of survival. Most of us do not want to put our families through that kind of emotional and financial drain. If you don't express your choice while you still can and appoint someone to act on your behalf, the decision is left with the government. Occasionally a doctor will guess at your choice, take pity on your family and allow nature to take its course. But fewer and fewer physicians are willing to take that risk in the face of potential civil and criminal legal proceedings against them.

We are not urging any of you to exercise your right to die. That is a personal decision that only you can make. What we are urging you to do is to make a choice. Don't let it go by default.

We believe that the Durable Power of Attorney for Health Care is your best hope of having a say about your medical care, including the exercise of the right to die, when you are no longer able to do so. Nothing is perfect, especially in such a delicate area as the preservation of human life, but if you don't at least attempt to get involved in these decisions, they will all be made for you and chances are that they will be made by hospital bureaucracies or by lawyers and judges or by some combination. Help yourself and your family by making these decisions in advance. This is one of the most important legal documents you could possibly have.

Directive to Physicians

If you do want to exercise your right to die, we also recommend that you sign a Directive to Physicians (sometimes called a Living Will). This is your own statement to your doctors that you do not want your life to be artificially sustained. It must be renewed every five years.

Chapter 7

What Do I Need for a Complete Estate Plan?

Nomination of Conservator of the Person

Your Living Trust provides for the management of your <u>assets</u> in case you become incompetent, but you may still need a conservator of your <u>person</u> in cases of certain incapacitating diseases such as Alzheimer's Disease. The Nomination of Conservator form allows you to choose the person who is charged with your physical care instead of having him or her chosen by the Probate Court.

Funeral and Burial Instructions Including Anatomical Gifts

We recommend that this be a separate document from your Pour Over Will. Your Pour Over Will, we would hope, will be a relatively insignificant document. It will only come into effect if you haven't done your job by transferring all your assets into your Living Trust during your lifetime.

We recommend that you keep all your Complete Estate Plan documents in a looseleaf notebook. This book should become a working book that's familiar to your spouse and your successor trustee. It is the family plan for the management of the family estate. Keeping the book up to date and keeping your co-trustee and successor trustee informed will make the administration of your estate at either death or incompetency as easy as is possible.

By having your Funeral and Burial Instructions as a separate document where your spouse and family know it will be, you save them the trouble of reading through longer documents at the most traumatic moment, right after your death. Most of us want to wait a bit after a loved one's passing to get involved with legal problems caused by the death. You also lessen the risk that the instructions inadvertently won't be read until after the funeral and burial.

Making your funeral and burial wishes known not only allows you to make the choice, it lifts a great burden from your family, who may not even all agree among themselves as to the best choice. There will be one less thing for them to worry about.

We believe that if you do want to make an anatomical gift that it's best to do it in this document. If all goes as planned, this will be the one document your family refers to right after death, while there is still time to make a gift.

Many of you, of course, will not choose to make an anatomical gift. That's fine. That's what a Complete Estate Plan is all about — exercising your choices.

Those who do want to make a gift usually have two concerns. First, are you too old to make a gift? The answer is that no one knows. Amazing things have

What Do I Need for a Complete Estate Plan?

been done with donations from elderly people. Moreover, medical science is making astounding advances in this field. If you want to make anatomical gift, go ahead and do it without regard to your age. Let the experts decide at the time of your death if the gift can be used. Don't predecide for them. Again, this is only if you want to make the gift in the first place.

The second concern is cost. Many who want to make an anatomical gift don't want to burden their family with the cost involved. There is no cause for concern. The cost of removing the organ and transporting it is billed to the hospital, which is reimbursed by Medicare.

Schedule of Assets

This is simply a list of all your assets inside your Living Trust. Remember, certain of your assets (most motor vehicles, a small checking account and retirement plans) are intentionally left outside the Living Trust, but your co-trustee or successor trustee will still want to know they exist. Keep a separate list of assets outside of your Living Trust.

We recommend that you review your Schedule of Assets at least once a year to make certain it is up to date and make certain that new assets were placed in the Living Trust.

Don't forget that the death benefits of your insurance policies are assets. We recommend that you make a copy of the facing page of all life insurance policies and keep them in your looseleaf notebook right after the Schedule of Assets. We also recommend that you also keep a copy of the grant deeds for all your real estate with your Schedule of Assets.

It's important to remember that just listing your assets on this schedule does not transfer them into your Living Trust. Each asset must be separately transferred.

Location Schedule

This document is intended to get your estate organized and ready to be administered. Take a look at each asset you have listed on your Schedule of Assets. For each asset, decide where the asset is located, what documents would be necessary to transfer the asset and where each document is located. Now make a record of each to keep in your looseleaf notebook. This is easier than it sounds because you are just fresh from transferring the assets into your Living Trust. Forming the Living Trust has forced you into getting yourself organized. The purpose of the Location Schedule is both to keep you organized in the future and to pass on this information to your co-trustee and successor trustee. We spoke

Chapter 7

What Do I Need for a Complete Estate Plan?

earlier of making your looseleaf notebook a "working" book, not just a "work" book. You will finally have a Complete Estate Plan when all of those who need to know can go right to the book and find your up-to-the-minute instructions for the administration of your estate. You need to work with it and not just hide it away. You've created a <u>Living</u> Trust that is meant to <u>involve</u> you and work for you during your life as well as after. As attorneys, we've seen all too many widows who were completely lost when their husbands died. "He always took care of our finances." He may have meant well, but he didn't take care of everything. He didn't prepare for the eventuality that he couldn't or wouldn't be around to "take care of everything." You're not doing your family any favors by keeping them in the dark. All you will be leaving them with is confusion and unnecessary legal and accounting bills to straighten things out.

The message is to get organized and pass the information along to those who need to know.

Instructions for Successor Trustee

This can be as simple as an instruction to contact the attorney who prepared the Living Trust for instructions or it can be the instructions themselves. We recommend that you obtain a general set of instructions from your attorney at the time you establish your Living Trust. These can be supplemented later for any particular problems your successor trustee may have when the issue arises.

Miscellaneous Other Trusts

There are a variety of other trusts that can be used in planning your estate. Most are applicable only in specialized situations or with very large estates. Just so you'll have familiarity with some of the names, we'll give you a brief description of some of the most commonly used estate planning trusts. The list is not meant to be exhaustive.

• <u>Insurance</u> <u>Trust</u>. This is a separate trust from your Living Trust. Most of you will probably not need an Insurance Trust, but it should always be considered as part of a Complete Estate Plan.

As you recall, death benefits from life insurance are includable in your net estate for estate tax purposes if you possess any incident of ownership of the policy or if the proceeds are payable to your estate. A properly drawn Insurance Trust keeps the insurance death benefits out of your estate for estate tax purposes.

If you are single and your net estate is more than $600,000 and part of the value of your estate comes from insurance

What Do I Need for a Complete Estate Plan?

death benefits, you should consider an Insurance Trust to supplement your Living Trust. If you are married and your net estate is more than $1,200,000 and part of the value of your estate comes from insurance death benefits, you should consider an Insurance Trust to supplement your A-B Living Trust or your A-B-C Living Trust.

In order to qualify for special tax treatment, the Insurance Trust, unlike the Living Trust, must be irrevocable. You, the trustor, create an irrevocable Insurance Trust, naming the Insurance Trust as the owner and beneficiary of your life insurance policies. You've made a gift of only the premium, which is normally excludable under the $10,000 per year per donee exclusion.

The apparent problem is that the trust is irrevocable and can't be changed. What if you want to change insurance policies? No problem. It's the trust that's irrevocable, not the insurance policy. If you want to change insurance policies, just stop paying the premium on the old policy and contribute a new policy to the Insurance Trust.

There are some disadvantages to the Insurance Trust. First, there is additional cost involved in establishing it. Secondly, the Insurance Trust must be irrevocable, but as we've seen, that should not be a major drawback since the insurance policies can still be cancelled. Thirdly, unlike the Living Trust, the trustor cannot be the trustee of the Insurance Trust. Fourth, it is recommended that you establish a separate bank account to make premium payments and that you make deposits into that account at different times and in different amounts than the amounts and times of the premium payments. Fifth, because of a recent court decision, you may not want to name your Living Trust as the beneficiary of the Insurance Trust.

Insurance is an obvious way to provide liquidity to pay estate taxes when your estate exceeds $600,000 as a single person or $1,200,000 as a married couple. The Insurance Trust, while it does have its drawbacks, can be a valuable tool to keep the proceeds of your insurance policies out of your taxable estate.

• Children's Trust. This is also a separate trust from your Living Trust. It should be considered by those of you with fairly large estates with appreciating assets that you don't need to live on.

The Children's Trust is an irrevocable trust with you as trustor and with your children or grandchildren as beneficiaries. Actually, the beneficiary could be anyone, but in almost of all cases the beneficiaries are the children or grand-

Chapter 7

What Do I Need for a Complete Estate Plan?

children of the trustors.

Whatever property you put into the Children's Trust is a gift to the beneficiaries. Remember, if the gift exceeds $10,000 per donor per donee per year ($20,000 per year per child for married couples), it starts to diminish your $600,000 ($1,200,000 for married couples with A-B Trusts or A-B-C Trusts) lifetime combined gift tax and estate tax exemption.

Once the asset is in the trust it cannot be withdrawn by you. Income goes to your children during the term of the trust and the principal goes to the children at whatever age you choose at the outset.

Prior to 1986, income was taxed at the child's lower tax rate, but now children under the age of fourteen are taxed at their parent's tax rate.

The major remaining benefit of the Children's Trust is to get what you anticipate to be an appreciating asset out of your estate while its value is relatively low, instead of at your death when you anticipate the value to be much higher. Think of your $600,000 or $1,200,000 unified gift and estate tax exemption as an account to draw on. Once you are overdrawn, your family starts getting taxed at rates ranging from 37% to 55%. You draw from your account every time you make a gift in excess of $10,000 per year per donee per donor or by leaving something in your estate. The object of the Children's Trust is to make a withdrawal from your account when the asset value is low instead of high.

Why use a trust rather than an outright gift? To delay distribution. If you make the gift to a Children's Trust, you control the asset until your children reach the age you choose for them to assume control. Meanwhile, the income from the trust, even though taxed at your rate, helps meet your obligation to maintain, support and educate your children. The disadvantage is that the Children's Trust must be irrevocable, so once the gift is made, it can't be taken back. The Children's Trust, like the Insurance Trust, is not for everyone, but it should be considered as part of a Complete Estate Plan.

• QDOT. If one or both spouses is not a U.S. citizen, their Living Trust should have special provisions making it a qualified domestic trust (usually called a QDOT).

In 1988 Congress decided to deny the unlimited marital deduction to the estate of a citizen spouse when assets pass to a non-citizen spouse. Congress felt that the surviving non-citizen spouse might take the assets and leave the

What Do I Need for a Complete Estate Plan?

United States to go back to his or her native land, and no estate taxes would ever be paid on the assets when the surviving spouse subsequently died.

The new law provides, however, that if the assets of the first spouse to die were placed in trust with a "qualified domestic trustee", such as a bank or other resident trustee, and such qualified domestic trustee became personally responsible for payment of estate taxes upon death of the surviving spouse, then the usual unlimited marital deduction would be allowed when the first spouse died.

Non-citizens and their spouses have to weigh the advantages of loss of control against the loss of the unlimited marital deduction. Congress also limited the amount that a citizen spouse can give to a non-citizen spouse without tax consequences to $100,000 per year instead of the usual unlimited gift tax exclusion between spouses.

• GRITS. This is the grantor retained income trust. It's used to make future gifts to others, but to retain the income to the donor.

• Totten Trust. This is the common bank account trust. The depositor maintains total control over the account during his or her life, but on the death of the depositor, the balance in the account goes to a named beneficiary automatically without any probate.

• Crummey Trust. This is a trust that allows the beneficiary to take all or any portion of the property placed in the trust up to the amount of the annual $10,000 exclusion for a limited number of years.

Now that we've described what we believe to be the Complete Estate Plan, let's see how well it meets our original objectives.

• Choice of heirs. The Letter of Instructions Regarding Personal Property allows you to designate how you want your personal effects to be distributed and the Living Trust designates how you want the rest of your estate distributed.

• Probate. If you transfer all your assets into the Living Trust (except for the few items we've mentioned), you will completely avoid probate. If you forget to transfer something into the Living Trust and become incompetent, your Durable General Power of Attorney will allow your attorney-in-fact to transfer the asset to the Living Trust for you.

Chapter 7

What Do I Need for a Complete Estate Plan?

The Complete Estate Plan

- The Living Trust

- Pour Over Will

- Assignment of Personal Property

- Letter of Instruction Regarding Personal Property

- Community Property Declaration

- Durable General Power of Attorney

- Durable Power of Attorney for Health Care

- Directive to Physicians

- Nomination of Conservator

- Funeral and Burial Instructions, Including Anatomical Gifts

- Schedule of Assets

- Location Schedule

- Instructions for Successor Trustee

What Do I Need for a Complete Estate Plan?

- Estate taxes. For single people, some of the miscellaneous trusts we've mentioned will minimize or eliminate estate taxes in some cases. The Living Trust will not affect a single person's estate taxes. For married people, the A-B Living Trust or the A-B-C Living Trust will eliminate or minimize estate taxes. The Pour Over Will will help make certain that all your assets go into the Living Trust at your death to take advantage of the A-B Trust or A-B-C Trust tax savings features. The other miscellaneous trusts we've mentioned will also minimize estate taxes for married couples where appropriate.

- Death Income Taxes. The Living Trust combined with the Community Property Declaration is the only way married couples can obtain the twin benefits of avoidance of probate and elimination of death income taxes at the same time. Joint tenancy avoids probate but only allows one-half the value of your property to be stepped-up in basis. Community property outside a Living Trust gives you the full step-up in basis but subjects you to the probate process.

- Conservatorship. Since your co-trustee or successor trustee can continue to manage the Living Trust without your signature should you become incompetent by invoking the incompetency clause, conservatorship will be avoided for management of your assets. The Durable General Power of Attorney also gives whomever you select power to act with regard to any property held outside the Living Trust. The Durable Power of Attorney for Health Care allows whomever you choose to make health care decisions in case you are unable to do so. The Nomination of Conservator selects a conservator of your person if you are unable to care for yourself physically.

- Control over assets. In many respects, this is the most important feature of the Complete Estate Plan. You and your family maintain control over your destinies -- not the government, not the courts, not lawyers, not accountants. The Living Trust allows you to continue to lead your life and control your assets just as you did before. Nothing becomes irrevocable until after the death of the first spouse to die, and then only as to the deceased spouse's portion. By avoiding probate, the Living Trust keeps your family in control of your assets after death and avoids the one to two year loss of control in the probate court.

What Do I Need for a Complete Estate Plan?

- <u>Flexibility</u>. Because the Living Trust is revocable, it can be modified, amended or even eliminated prior to death.

- <u>Privacy</u>. Two of the greatest possible intrusions on your personal privacy are probate and conservatorship. All of your business suddenly becomes the public's business. Your life becomes a public record. Judges, lawyers and accountants are unnecessarily drawn into your life. While the expense and frustration of delay are usually cited as the primary evils of probate and conservatorship, loss of privacy is equally or even more important in some people's eyes. The Living Trust is the only estate planning tool that avoids both conservatorship and probate and maintains your right to privacy. There is a specific right to privacy written into the California Constitution, and the United States Supreme Court has interpreted the U.S. Constitution to give all U.S. citizens a right to privacy. Tell that to anyone who's been through a probate or a conservatorship. Probate/conservatorship and privacy are mutually inconsistent terms.

- <u>Health care</u>. Your Durable Power of Attorney for Health Care allows your nominee to make health care decisions for you when you can't. The law requires that you renew this document every seven years. Your Directive to Physicians must be renewed every five years. We recommend that you make at least an annual review of the Complete Estate Plan to make sure it's current and to keep those who need to know in the know. Your annual review should remind you to renew your Durable Power of Attorney for Health Care and Directive to Physicians, as needed, but if you're in a situation where you anticipate a future incapacity and your Durable Power of Attorney for Health Care or Directive to Physicians is nearing expiration, don't wait to renew. Once incompetent you no longer have the power to renew.

- <u>Funeral and burial instructions</u>. Your Complete Estate Plan assists your family by separating these instructions from other legal documents. Your instructions are less likely to be ignored or overlooked, and you will save your family from going through your legal papers until after the funeral. If you follow our suggestion and put your Complete Estate Plan documents in a looseleaf book and making that book a "working" book to be periodically reviewed by those who need to know, your funeral and burial in-

What Do I Need for a Complete Estate Plan?

structions will be easily found before it's too late.

- <u>Anatomical gifts</u>. If you follow our advice and make this a part of your funeral and burial instructions, your wishes, no matter what they may be, have the highest likelihood of being followed.

- <u>Administration of estate</u>. The secret of the Complete Estate Plan is that you've already done 90% of the work of administering your estate before you die. You are the person who can do it best. You know what and where your assets are. You know where your important papers are. You know to whom you want to have your assets go. You don't need probate courts, executors and lawyers to do this for you. Most estates using the Complete Estate Plan can be settled in a matter of days rather than in one to two years. By your proper planning you have made the administration of your estate as quick, simple and inexpensive as possible.

Chapter 8

How Do I Establish a Complete Estate Plan?

If you've read this far, we're sure you're at least interested in a Living Trust and probably in a Complete Estate Plan, but you're also probably concerned about the effort, time and expense involved. In this chapter we intend to show you how to go about planning your estate and give you some estimates of the time, effort and expense in establishing and implementing your plan.

There are five steps involved in planning your estate:

- Choose an attorney.
- Prepare for meeting with your attorney.
- Meet with your attorney.
- Review, complete and sign documents prepared by your attorney.
- Put assets into your Living Trust.

Choose An Attorney

Your first question might be whether you really need an attorney at all. There are people called estate planners or financial planners who aren't attorneys who put together estate plans and there are also do-it-yourself books. The simple answer is that you are dealing with what are probably the most important legal documents you will ever be involved with. They are designed to deal with and dispose of <u>all</u> of your assets and to give you the peace of mind of knowing that you've made complete and proper plans for your estate. Only a major lawsuit, a divorce or a sale of your business would rival the legal importance of an estate plan. You wouldn't go to your dentist for brain surgery or, for that matter, rely on a do-it-yourself book (if you do, it at least proves the point that you needed the brain surgery).

To carry the analogy further, you also don't go to your family physician for brain surgery, you go to a specialist. Here lies the problem. You need to find a lawyer specializing in estate planning. But even

Chapter 8

How Do I Establish a Complete Estate Plan?

then, you have to make sure that your attorney is ready, willing and able to prepare a Living Trust for you and not go the traditional route of a will, or a will and a testamentary trust.

Almost all lawyers know how to prepare wills. But even some who do know how won't prepare them because they've chosen to limit their practice to another specialty, such as personal injury lawsuits. Usually only lawyers who specialize in estate planning will prepare testamentary trusts. Almost all lawyers who call themselves estate planning specialists will advise you to have either a will or a will with a testamentary trust, without even considering or, often, even telling you about the Living Trust.

There are three basic reasons for this: (1) tradition, (2) ignorance, and (3) self-interest.

Lawyers, even more than most people, are creatures of tradition. Precedent is the cornerstone of our legal system. Most people who plan their estate use wills and testamentary trusts. It's been that way for centuries. It works. Why change? Tradition is a powerful force in the thinking of the legal profession.

Many lawyers also know little or nothing about the Living Trust. They don't recommend it because they don't know how well it works. In the past the Living Trust was used primarily by the wealthy, who could afford the most sophisticated and creative attorneys. John F. Kennedy and Bing Crosby are good examples. The average attorney was taught wills and testamentary trusts in law school and has rarely, if ever, had the occasion to study the Living Trust.

The third reason some attorneys do not recommend the Living Trust is their own self-interest. This is unfortunate, but, sadly enough, true in some cases. A friend used to say that it's a shame that the 96% of worthless attorneys spoil it for the other 4%, but we won't go that far. Most attorneys will prepare a will for you for a very modest fee. If so, it's not done out of generosity. It's a loss leader for the future probate, where the fees can be very rewarding. The best of all possible worlds for an estate planning attorney is the will with a testamentary trust. The work involved justifies a more substantial fee than for just a will, and then later the probate fees will still be coming in. Unfortunately for the client, he or she could have had a Living Trust for the same or even less of a fee than for the will and testamentary trust and then could forget about probate fees forever.

The problems of tradition and ignorance can be overcome. They're really just two branches of the same problem — a failure of education. The Living

How Do I Establish a Complete Estate Plan?

Trust, in fact, has a tradition just as long as the testamentary trust. It has worked, and worked well, for centuries. It is recognized in all 50 states and by the IRS. Unfortunately, it is only being used by approximately one percent of the American public. The real problem is one of education. We must educate the legal profession about the little known, but time-honored, tool to solve their clients' estate planning problems and we must educate the American public to demand the Living Trust instead of just the standard estate planning package.

Of course, if you have an attorney who's acting in his or her own self interest and not yours, education won't work. We would like to believe that that won't happen often (well, we would <u>like</u> to believe it). If you have an attorney who just needs to be educated, you've got an honest lawyer, but you don't have the one who should plan your estate. Legal educations are very expensive. They're expensive for the lawyer's family before he or she passes the bar, and they're expensive for the lawyer's clients after he or she passes the bar. Legal fees commonly range between $100 and $200 per hour. (Actually they're often substantially higher for large corporations, which are able to pass them back to us as consumers in higher prices.) But even at the very lowest end of the scale, $100

per hour adds up fast when even the most well intentioned, diligent and efficient attorney has to learn a new area of the law and then create complex legal documents that both carry out your wishes and comply with all local, state and federal laws, rules and regulations.

All this is just another way of saying that you need to find a lawyer who's ready, willing and able to provide you with a high quality Living Trust at a reasonable price — one who specializes in the Living Trust.

Basically there are two ways to find any specialist: referrals and interviews. If you know someone who has a Living Trust, ask him or her who prepared it, how long it took, what it cost and how satisfied he or she was with the attorney. If you get satisfactory responses, call the attorney's office, but instead of just making an appointment, go through the interview process we recommend.

We recommend this interview process whether you're coming to an attorney by a referral or otherwise. First of all, if you're looking for a specialist in the Living Trust, the attorney's office staff ought to be able to answer all preliminary questions and set up an appointment with the attorney. If the office staff can't answer these questions, the office probably does not specialize in the Living Trust.

Chapter 8

How Do I Establish a Complete Estate Plan?

The first question is easy and obvious. "Does your office specialize in the Living Trust?" Don't bother to ask if the office specializes in estate planning. A positive answer doesn't help because you're just going to have to ask about Living Trusts next anyway. Attorneys who specialize in the Living Trust will have a staff that knows that that's what they do. If they're not certain, they're not for you. Ask to see if they can refer you to someone who does specialize in the Living Trust.

If you get a positive response to our first question, ask "Approximately how many Living Trusts has your office prepared?" You need to know how much experience these people have. Our office, for example, has prepared over 9,000 Living Trusts. Experience is the key to quality work at a reasonable price.

If you get responses that sound like the attorney you've reached has a staff that knows that their office specializes in the Living Trust and knows that their office has substantial experience in preparing Living Trusts, next ask "What will it cost for an initial consultation with the attorney?" You need to know this so there will be no misunderstanding. As we've stated, hourly rates for attorneys commonly range between $100 per hour and $200 per hour. Some charge for the initial consultation and others don't. For example, our office offers a free initial consultation of one-half hour. If you are getting a free initial consultation, also establish how long it will be. It's only fair to the attorney not to take up any more time than offered if you decide not to go forward, and it will also help you budget your own time in preparing for the meeting. Whether or not you are being charged on an hourly basis for the initial meeting, it's extremely important to be well organized for the first meeting. We'll discuss how to get organized later.

If the initial consultation is either free or an amount you consider reasonable, ask "If I decide to go forward with a Living Trust, what will it cost me?" Again, you don't want any surprises down the road. If the answer is quoted in an hourly rate, you've got the wrong attorney. Many legal services have to be quoted in hourly rates because no one knows at the outset how much time is going to be involved. For example, some divorces are simple and take only a few hours and others are either bitter or complex or both and take hundreds or even thousands of hours. An attorney can't reasonably quote a fixed fee because he or she has no idea at the outset what the other side is going to do. A fixed fee low enough to be fair to the client might mean that the lawyer has to

How Do I Establish a Complete Estate Plan?

work hours and hours for free (you get less than enthusiastic legal representation under these circumstances). On the other hand, a fixed fee high enough to be fair to the attorney might mean that the client with a simple case is being grossly overcharged for the amount of effort being put in by the attorney. This is not unlike the fixed fee schedule for attorneys in probate. Only in probate, the attorney has an escape hatch. If the fixed fee isn't high enough, he or she can always petition the Probate Court for "extraordinary" fees.

Preparation of a Living Trust is not like a divorce or any other matter where even an experienced attorney cannot reasonably estimate the amount of time it will take. If the office you've contacted will only quote you an hourly fee, it means either that they are not experienced enough to know how much time it will take to complete the project or that they're concerned that the size of the fee you're going to be charged will scare you away.

To give you a reference point on fees, we'll give you an example of what our office charges as of the time this book is being written. Be aware that fees do change from time to time, so always feel free to call our office at (415) 776-5100 to get an idea of current rates. We currently charge a fixed fee of $800 for single

people with an A Trust and a fixed fee of $900 for a married couple with either an A Trust or an A-B Trust (the charge is per couple, not per person). There are additional fixed charges if you want an A-B-C Trust, an Insurance Trust, a Children's Trust or any of the other miscellaneous trusts.

If you are quoted a fixed fee that makes sense to you, the next very important question is "What's included in the fixed fee?" Here's where you must decide how much of the Complete Estate Plan you want or need. Remember, the Living Trust is by far the most important element in the Complete Estate Plan, but you should at least consider all of the other elements we discussed in Chapter Seven. For example, our office believes that many of the documents we've discussed are so important that we currently include them with every Living Trust at no additional charge. The documents included as part of our basic estate plan are:

- The Living Trust (A Trust or A-B Trust)
- The Pour Over Will
- A Community Property Declaration (if you are married)
- A Durable General Power of Attorney
- A Durable Power of Attorney for Health Care

Chapter 8

How Do I Establish a Complete Estate Plan?

- A Directive to Physicians
- A Nomination of Conservator
- A Grant Deed for one parcel of real estate, including the documents to exclude the transfer from Proposition 13 reassessment and from transfer taxes
- An Assignment of Personal Property into the Living Trust
- An Instruction Letter for the disposition of your personal property after your death
- An Instruction Letter showing you how to transfer assets into the Living Trust
- An Instruction Letter for the successor trustee after the death of the Trustors
- A Schedule of Assets
- A Location Schedule
- Funeral and Burial Instructions Including an Anatomical Gift

If you own more than one parcel of real estate in California, we currently charge $50 for preparing the documents for transferring each additional parcel. Out of state transfers will have to be handled separately in each state by local attorneys. You are responsible for recording all deeds and paying the recording fees (usually $9.00). You are also responsible for completing and signing the documents we provide and transferring your property to the Living Trust pursuant to the instructions we provide.

Only if you want or need an A-B-C Trust, an Insurance Trust, a Children's Trust or any other miscellaneous trusts are there any additional charges.

We currently require a $500 retainer deposit if you want us to go forward with the preparation of your documents at the end of the initial meeting, with the balance due when we complete the documents and review them with you at a second meeting.

We are going over our current fee arrangements in detail to show you that: (1) it is possible to set fixed fees for estate planning; (2) you need not be embarrassed about obtaining a precise understanding about fees before you commit yourself; and (3) it is absolutely essential that you know exactly what is included in the fixed fee and what, if any, extra charges will be involved.

Once you determine that the attorney's fee structure is satisfactory to you and that you'll be getting all of the documents you want, make an appointment and ask what you should bring with you. We'll discuss this separately next in conjunction with our suggestions on how to prepare for the initial meeting, but make sure you ask the question so you'll know what your prospective attorney wants you to bring to the meeting.

One word about the appointment, you should make every effort to be on time

How Do I Establish a Complete Estate Plan?

and to give as much advance warning as possible if you have to cancel. The only way attorneys who specialize in Living Trusts can keep fees reasonable and in reach of everyone is to operate efficiently. As Lincoln said, "Time is an attorney's stock in trade. It is all he has to sell." Unfortunately, it's a perishable commodity. Once lost, it's lost forever (unless you really believe in all those time-travel movies).

Preparation For Meeting

Now that you've found a law office that specializes in the preparation of Living Trusts and has a fee arrangement that you both understand and find acceptable, it's time to prepare for the initial meeting so that you will be able to answer all of your attorney's questions and provide him or her with necessary documents.

First, you need to make an estimate of your net worth, both with and without insurance death benefits included. If you're single, make sure your gross net worth exceeds or will exceed $60,000, and you'll know you're a candidate for the Living Trust. If you're single and own a significant amount of insurance, you will also want to consider an Insurance Trust if your net estate, including insurance death benefits, will exceed $600,000 at the time of your death.

For married couples, it's essential to estimate your net worth in determining whether to select the A Trust, the A-B Trust, the A-B-C Trust or any additional trusts.

Remember, you're trying to make a prediction of your net estate at the time of your death. Take your best estimate of the current fair market value of all of your assets and subtract all of your liabilities. The hard part, of course, is to try to predict the future and decide what it's all likely to be worth when you pass away and, if you're married, when your spouse passes away. This is a function of too many things to make precise predictions. You can't predict the future, but you can make intelligent estimates. If you arc still working, your estate is more likely to grow than if you are retired. The longer you have to live, the more likely that your estate will grow. Plus, remember the statistic that the surviving spouse lives an average of ten years after the first to die. Then there's the inflation factor. We're lawyers and not economists, but our guess is that we'll have continued inflation whether the government officially admits it or not. If your guess is the same as ours, add an inflation factor to your assets over your estimated lifetime. The easiest rate of inflation to work with mathematically is seven percent, because it doubles all values every ten years.

How Do I Establish a Complete Estate Plan?

Effects of Inflation on an Estate's Value

Inflation Rate	Years to Double
5%	14
6%	12
7%	10
8%	9
9%	8
10%	7
11%	6-1/2
12%	6

How Do I Establish a Complete Estate Plan?

Once you have your estimated net estate, you should be able to make a good decision as to whether you need an A Trust, an A-B Trust or an A-B-C Trust. You will also need to know the death benefits on your insurance policies to see if you should consider an Insurance Trust. Remember there are some reasons that a married couple may want to select an A-B Trust even if their gross estate is currently under $600,000.

The main point is to get a handle on your net worth estimates and insurance death benefit values so you and your attorney can decide which trust is most appropriate for you at your initial meeting.

If you are married, you next need to determine if any of your property is separate property. In general, if you owned it prior to your marriage, it was given to you or you inherited it and you have not commingled it with your community property, it is your separate property. If you have separate property, you need to decide if you want to keep it as separate property or convert it to community property. We've already discussed the advantages and disadvantages of converting separate property to community property.

You should next consider the distribution of your property at death. Almost all, but certainly not all, married couples leave everything to the surviving spouse and then, at the death of the surviving spouse, everything remaining is equally divided among the children. Even if that is your choice, you still have two more basic decisions. First, if one of your children predeceases the surviving spouse, do you want his or her share to go to his or her spouse, his or her children or back to be redivided among your other children — or some other way. The other basic choice you need to make is whether or not to delay distribution to your children. Do your adult children, even if they're only eighteen, get it all right away or do you want to delay some or all of the distribution to when they're more mature?

Remember, whether you're married or single, you can pick any distribution pattern you want. The worst place to think about this for the first time is in your lawyer's office. It's entirely appropriate to discuss all of this with your lawyer and to get his or her advice, but it's far better to have thought it through prior to the first meeting.

Next, you should decide who is going to fill the important positions of: (1) successor trustee of your Living Trust; (2) executor of your Pour Over Will; (3) guardian of your minor and incapacitated adult children, if any; (4) attorney-in-fact for your Durable Powers of Attorney;

Chapter 8

How Do I Establish a Complete Estate Plan?

What Happens if a Beneficiary Predeceases You?
The Choice is up to You

Husband and wife have two children, Bob and Sue. Bob and Sue are each married. Bob has two children, and Sue has three.

Husband and wife leave their entire estate to the survivor of the two of them and then at the death of the survivor, the estate is to be equally divided between Bob and Sue.

Unexpectedly, the sequence of death is first husband, then Bob and then wife. How is the estate divided?

Typical Choices

- Sue receives 1/2 and Bob's two children each receive 1/4; or
- Sue receives everything.

Unusual Choices

- Sue receives 1/2 and Bob's widow receives 1/2; or
- Sue receives 1/3 and Bob's two children receive 1/3 each.

What if Sue and Bob both predeceased their parents?

Typical Choices

- Bob's two children each receive 1/4 and Sue's three childen each receive 1/6; or
- The five grandchildren each receive 1/5.

and (5) conservator of your person. The usual pattern for married couples is to pick the spouse to fill all roles initially where appropriate and to pick the person you choose as successor trustee of your Living Trust to fill all other roles in the event your spouse cannot. As you have seen, the person you select as successor trustee must be someone you trust. If you trust that person enough to be your successor trustee, you probably trust that person enough to make other major decisions. But the choice is up to you. The virtue of estate planning is that you make the choices. Remember, if you don't, the government will.

This is not absolutely necessary, but it is extremely helpful to your attorney if you bring to the first meeting a typed or printed list of the name, address and telephone number of yourself and all people who you're considering to receive any portion of your estate, to be your successor trustee, to be guardian, etc. This will save a lot of time and help prevent misspellings in the final documents.

Next you should obtain copies of the grant deeds to any real estate you might own. You will want to bring copies to your attorney rather than the originals. Your attorney will need these to prepare new grant deeds to transfer the property to the Living Trust. Remember, it's the grant deed and not the deed

of trust that's needed. The grant deed is the document that transferred the property from the previous owner to you. The deed of trust is the document the lender required to allow it to take your property from you should you stop making those monthly payments. You should also bring the current real estate tax bill for your property so that the identification number of your real property can be determined.

Next, you should locate any previous wills and trusts that you have signed and bring them along to the initial meeting.

The last two items you'll need to bring to the first meeting are your spouse and your checkbook. Most attorneys will require a retainer deposit to begin work and, unless your spouse is incapacitated, you should both attend the meeting.

Meeting With Your Attorney

Every meeting with every attorney takes a slightly different format. We'll try to generalize about what a typical meeting might be like from our own experience.

The first surprise might be that you may not be meeting with an attorney at all. More and more law offices are using "paralegals" to perform tasks that were traditionally performed by attorneys. The law requires that only attorneys (and

Chapter 8

How Do I Establish a Complete Estate Plan?

Checklist for Meeting with Attorney

- Have an estimate of your net worth.

- Know the death benefit of your life insurance, if any.

- Bring a list of any separate property owned by either spouse, if married.

- Bring a copy of grant deed and tax bill for all real estate owned.

- Know how you want your estate to be distributed, both on your death and on spouse's death, if married.

- Know if you want to delay distribution of your estate until the beneficiaries reach specified ages.

- Know who you want to be your co-trustee, successor trustee, executor, attorney-in-fact, guardian of your children and conservator of your person. Bring a printed or typed list of their names, addresses and telephone numbers.

- Bring previously executed wills and trusts.

- Bring your spouse, if married.

- Bring your check book.

How Do I Establish a Complete Estate Plan?

in a few special cases, law students) can appear in court for a client, and only an attorney can give legal advice. What constitutes legal advice is often a matter of dispute. Anyone can call themselves a paralegal. No special training is required, and there is no licensing requirement for paralegals. Some paralegals have been carefully trained and have sufficient experience at what they're doing to do specific tasks as well as, or often better than, an attorney who has little or no experience in that particular field. For example, much of the work done by law firms in probate cases is actually performed by probate paralegals rather than by attorneys. Your law firm may or may not make you aware of that fact.

We believe that all client meetings for estate planning should be conducted by an attorney. In our office an attorney will always attend all client conferences. We want to make certain that your documents accurately reflect your decisions and that all of your questions are answered properly. While some paralegals are excellent at what they do, we still recommend that you make certain that the person you're meeting with is an attorney and not a paralegal.

Most of the early part of the meeting will involve questions by the attorney to determine your present marital status, whether you've been married before, whether you have children from this or a prior marriage, whether or not you have separate property and, if so, if you want to convert any of it to community property, how you want your estate distributed on your death, your net worth, etc. After gathering this information, the attorney should be able to determine with you whether you need an A Trust, an A-B Trust, or an A-B-C Trust and also decide whether or not you want to consider any other trusts.

After the attorney makes a recommendation to you, you should ask whatever questions you may have that haven't already been answered. At this time make certain that you know exactly what services the attorney is proposing, when the attorney can complete the project and what the fee will be. Even though you may have discussed the fee with a member of the attorney's staff prior to the meeting, make sure that you and the attorney discuss fees again and that you completely understand the charges and are agreeable with the amount proposed to be charged. If there is any discrepancy between what you understood from the telephone conversation and what you are told at this meeting, bring it up right away. The best time to resolve problems with fees is at the beginning and not at the end.

Chapter 8

How Do I Establish a Complete Estate Plan?

If you are in agreement on what is to be done, on the amount of the fee, on how long it will take and are comfortable with the attorney, tell him or her to proceed with completing your documents. Most attorneys will ask for a retainer at this point. Some may request payment in full in advance. The current policy in our office is to require a retainer deposit of $500 at this point. As you will see when you get your documents, there is a lot of work to be done. The retainer is to make certain that you are serious about going forward with your estate plan. If at the end of this meeting you are not certain about going forward, you should do yourself and the attorney a favor and admit it. Don't pay the retainer, and don't have the attorney do a lot of unnecessary work. We believe that planning your estate is one of the most important things you can possibly do for yourself and your family. When you do it, you should do it right.

If all has gone well to this point, you should set an appointment for your next meeting to review and sign what your attorney is going to prepare for you. Usually this is two to three weeks away, but if you have any special time problems, most attorneys will be able to expedite the process.

In our experience, this first meeting should take from one-half hour to forty-five minutes.

Review, Complete and Sign Documents

The purpose of the second meeting with your attorney should be to review and sign some of the documents that have been prepared for you and to obtain instructions on how to complete the other documents and on how to transfer your property into your Living Trust.

If you are married, both you and your spouse should attend this second meeting as well. In our office we like to get as many of the documents as possible actually signed and notarized at the second meeting, but your attorney may have a different policy on this.

You want to make certain that the documents accurately reflect your desires. There are basically three ways for an attorney to have you review the documents: (1) mail them to you in advance of the meeting; (2) give them to you at the meeting and have you review them there; or (3) give them to you at the meeting and have you review them at your leisure.

In our office, we actually use a blend of the last two alternatives. We don't mail in advance because the papers are formal legal documents that do need some explanation. At our second meeting we go over the papers with you and make

How Do I Establish a Complete Estate Plan?

certain that they reflect your desires, but we don't ask you to go over them in detail under any kind of time pressure. After they have been explained to you, you can read them at leisure at home. Our current policy is that for the next two weeks you can telephone us with any questions and request any changes to the documents at no charge. Every law office will have its own policy on this, so make sure you understand it.

In our office we like to have the Living Trust, the Pour Over Will, the Community Property Declaration, the Assignment of Personal Property, the Directive to Physicians, the Grant Deeds (including documents necessary to exempt the transfer from Proposition 13 reassessment and from transfer taxes), the Durable Powers of Attorney and Nomination of Conservator all executed, witnessed and notarized at the second meeting if at all possible. (If you have chosen to have any other trust, such as an Insurance Trust, we complete these at a later time.) We then leave it to you to record the Grant Deeds and to complete the Schedule of Assets, the Location Schedule and the Funeral and Burial Instructions Including Anatomical Gifts at your convenience. You should be able to complete these documents in about an hour after the second meeting. If you have any questions, you're free to call our office at no charge for the next two weeks.

Part of the materials we give to you at the first meeting is a set of instructions on how to transfer your property, other than the real estate we've taken care of, to the Living Trust. Take a look at Appendix J at the back of the book. It contains most of our instructions. You might ask why we don't also take care of this for you as well. The answer is one of efficiency and cost. Unlike real property transfers, no special legal skill is required to make these transfers. With our instructions, you can do this as well, if not better, than we can. Some of you will have a great deal of property to transfer and others will have little. We could do this for you, but we see no reason why you should pay legal fees for something you can do yourself. One of the goals of the Complete Estate Plan is to encourage self-help and to discourage the unnecessary use of attorneys whenever possible.

In any event, no matter what law firm you use, you should be clear at the end of the second meeting as to: (1) what is completed; (2) what still needs to be done; and (3) who is going to do each item that still needs to be done.

In our office, we like to have duplicate executed copies, one set for our files and one set for you. No matter what law

How Do I Establish a Complete Estate Plan?

firm you use, make sure that you get an originally executed copy of each document for yourself. This is <u>your</u> estate plan, and you and your family are actively involved in it. It's not like a will that gathers dust in a lawyer's safe until probate time.

This second meeting should typically last approximately forty-five to sixty minutes. At the conclusion of the meeting most attorneys, including myself, will ask that you pay the balance due on the fixed fee. Ask the attorney if he or she can allocate a portion of the bill to tax planning. A portion of this may be deductible on your income tax return. Unfortunately this is usually not the case for single people, since they all end up with the A Trust. If the attorney is willing to make the allocation, ask him or her to put it right on your statement or receipt so you will have it at   tax time.

Transfer Assets to Living Trust

Remember, you're not finished after the second meeting. You must record your grant deeds and you must transfer the rest of your assets into the Living Trust.

Recording the grant deeds is easy, but you must remember that each grant deed must be recorded in the county recorder's office in which the property is located. For example, if you own a home in San Carlos and some investment property in Petaluma, you must record the deed to your home in the San Mateo County Recorder's Office in Redwood City and the deed to your investment property in the Sonoma County Recorder's Office in Santa Rosa. If you're not sure of the location of the county recorder's office, try your telephone book or call information for the address. Recordation of your deeds can be done by mail, but we find it's easier in the long run to meet the bureaucracy face-to-face and deal with whatever problems they're having that day rather than getting back cryptic form letters relating some problem you won't be able to understand. The usual recorder's fee is $9.00, but you might want to call in advance to check it out because fees change from time to time on a county by county basis. If you have any problems recording your deeds that aren't easily solved, you should call the attorney who prepared them for assistance. If the problem was the attorney's fault, he or she should not charge you for correcting it.

Keep remembering that one of the primary reasons that you established your Living Trust was to avoid probate, and you won't avoid probate on any asset you don't put in the trust, so get busy right away and get the job done. Read what your attorney has given you about

How Do I Establish a Complete Estate Plan?

how each type of asset is to be transferred. If you don't understand something, call and get it clarified. Don't leave an asset outside the Living Trust just because you don't understand how to get it transferred.

The goal for John Doe and Mary Doe, who signed their Living Trust on March 1, 1990, is to get all their assets (except a small bank account, most motor vehicles and their retirement plans) that have formal legal title (title that's registered in someone's records) held as follows: "John Doe and Mary Doe, Trustees, U.D.T., dated March 1, 1990."

Remember, items of personal property like your personal effects, jewelry and household furniture, don't have formal legal title registered with anyone. Those items are transferred to your Living Trust by an Assignment of Personal Property form that should just be kept with your other estate planning documents.

Once you have completed all of the documents your attorney prepared for you and transferred all your assets to your Living Trust, you have completed the initial process. Your job now is to: (1) remember to acquire all new assets in the name of the Living Trust; (2) review your Complete Estate Plan documents at least annually to see that they still meet your needs and desires and

that you've remembered to put all new assets into the Living Trust; (3) keep your co-trustee and successor trustee up to date on your estate plan; and (4) renew your Durable Power of Attorney for Health Care every seven years and your Directive to Physicians every five years.

Occasionally there will be a change in the law that will require that your documents be amended. The last major change in the law that required that all estate planning documents be reviewed and amended occurred in 1981. You should have an understanding with your attorney that he or she will notify you of any change in the law requiring amendment of your documents.

If you find your situation or desires have changed after your documents have been prepared, call your attorney. Many changes on the less formal documents, such as your Funeral and Burial Instructions, can be made by you, without an attorney. Changes to your more formal documents, such as the Living Trust or the Pour Over Will, will require your attorney to prepare an amendment or a codicil.

Since you now have your Complete Estate Plan up and running, let's look at how well it can work for you in our next chapter.

Chapter 9

How Will My Complete Estate Plan Work in Life and Death Situations?

To see how a Complete Estate Plan is meant to work during your life and after your death, let's take a look at a married couple, Jack and Jill Hill, with a 23 year old daughter, Joan, and a 17 year old son, Jim. Jack and Jill have a gross estate of $1,200,000 and a net estate of $1,000,000.

After reading this book Jack and Jill found an attorney specializing in Living Trusts and established a Complete Estate Plan. Because of the size of their net estate, they chose an A-B Living Trust. Jack and Jill were co-trustees of the Living Trust, and Joan was named as successor trustee. The distribution of the estate was to be all to the surviving spouse and upon the death of the surviving spouse, equally divided between Joan and Jim, with distribution of principal delayed until each child reaches age 30.

Jack chose Jill as the executor of his Pour Over Will, his attorney in fact for his Durable Powers of Attorney and his nominee for conservator. Jill also designated Jack to fill the same functions for her. Both Jack and Jill selected Joan to act as a successor trustee under the Living Trust and as successor executor, successor attorney-in-fact and successor nominee for conservator. Both Jack and Jill chose Jill's sister Jane as guardian for Jim in case both of them should die before Jim reached 18 years of age.

Jack and Jill owned a home, with a mortgage, two cars, some stocks and bonds, a savings account, a checking account, Jack's IRA and a $100,000 life insurance policy on Jack's life. After they established their Living Trust, the Hills deeded their house to themselves as trustees of their Living Trust, with no reassessment of their home for property tax purposes and no transfer taxes. They transferred their stocks and bonds to the Living Trust with a simple letter to their broker, following the instruction letter

How Will My Complete Estate Plan Work in Life and Death Situations?

given to them by their attorney. They went to the bank and transferred title to their savings account to their Living Trust, but left their joint checking account in joint tenancy. In checking the title on their cars, they noticed that one vehicle was registered Jack's name and the other was in Jill's name. They went to the DMV and changed title to both vehicles to Jack or Jill Hill. They next changed the beneficiary of Jack's life insurance policy to the Living Trust, with Joan as contingent beneficiary (just in case the Living Trust was ever terminated for some reason). Joan was left as Jack's primary beneficiary on the IRA, but the Living Trust was added as the contingent beneficiary.

Neither Jack nor Jill owned any separate property, but they completed their Community Property Declaration to make it absolutely clear that their home, which was formerly in their names as joint tenants, was in fact their community property, as was all of the rest of their property.

Jack and Jill then completed their Schedule of Assets by listing all of their assets and also completed their Location Index. Just to make their working book complete, they also inserted copies of the face page of their life insurance policy, a copy of the grant deed to their home, copies of brokerage statements for

their stocks and bonds, a copy of their savings passbook and a copy of the mutual fund statement for Jack's IRA.

After they completed their Funeral and Burial Instructions and decided that they preferred not to make any anatomical gifts, Jack and Jill sat down with Joan and explained what was in the working book and where it could be located. They also gave Joan the name, address and telephone number of the attorney who had prepared the documents and a copy of the Instructions to Successor Trustee that the attorney had provided.

From there on, Jack and Jill went on with their business just as they had before. Once every year or so they reviewed their Complete Estate Plan to make certain it still fit their needs and that any new assets purchased during the last year had been obtained in the name of their Living Trust. During one review, Jill changed her mind and decided that she did want to make an anatomical gift. She called her attorney and discovered that she could change the document herself without the attorney's assistance.

Each year at income tax time, Jack and Jill continued to file their joint returns on Form 1040 under their own social security numbers.

Once, when the Hills decided to refinance their home, they did have to take

How Will My Complete Estate Plan Work in Life and Death Situations?

their house out of their Living Trust briefly to satisfy the lender, but the title company provided them with the documents to put it right back into the Living Trust as part of the closing papers. Other than that, life went on pretty much as it had before the Hills decided to plan their estate.

Unfortunately, five years later, Jack was in a serious automobile accident. His car had fallen down a hill, causing serious brain damage and leaving him in a coma. At first, Jill was distraught and did nothing but visit Jack in the hospital. One day Joan came to the hospital with a letter to Jack and Jill from a stock brokerage firm where Jack had just transferred their account. Unfortunately, Jack had forgotten to tell the new broker about the Living Trust.

Even in her distressed state, Jill remembered that it was important to make sure that their stocks and bonds were in the name of the Living Trust and not their own names. When Jill called the brokerage firm she was told that since she couldn't get Jack's signature to transfer the account, she would have to hire an attorney to go to court and have herself appointed as Jack's conservator so she could sign on his behalf.

Jill remembered that one of the reasons she and Jack had established a Living Trust was to avoid conservatorship, but she got concerned when she read the incompetency clause of her Living Trust. It only works for assets that are in the Living Trust. What about their stocks and bonds that were accidentally left outside the Living Trust?

Fortunately, Jill came across the Durable General Power of Attorney in her working book, which reminded her that she had the power acting alone, when Jack was incompetent, to transfer the entire brokerage account to the Living Trust, which she promptly did. All she needed to do was send the brokerage firm a copy of her Durable General Power of Attorney and an instruction letter.

During the several weeks that followed Jack's accident, Jill was able to manage all of the family's financial affairs without ever having to involve herself with court procedures because the incompetency clause of her Living Trust allowed her to completely avoid conservatorship.

While things were going fine on the financial front (Jack was still covered on his group medical policy for a few more months of care), Jack's medical condition continued to deteriorate. Effectively, he was brain dead and just being kept alive on a respirator. Jill remembered her discussions with Jack and knew that Jack did not want to extend his own suffering or the anguish of his

Chapter 9

How Will My Complete Estate Plan Work in Life and Death Situations?

family, and also he did not want to bankrupt his family when his medical insurance benefits ran out. As difficult as it was, Jill exercised her powers under Jack's Durable Power of Attorney for Health Care to allow Jack's decision to stand.

Jill had been through their Complete Estate Plan working book many times and knew exactly what was in Jack's Funeral and Burial Instructions, but she decided to double check just to make certain that she had recalled properly. It was a relief that she didn't have to go through all of Jack's papers right away to find his Funeral and Burial Instructions. It was a reminder to Jill that she should make certain to keep Joan up to date on the working book now that Jack was gone. But all that could wait until after the funeral.

Since Joan was her successor trustee, Jill decided to have her assist her in settling Jack's affairs. Jill and Joan reviewed the Instructions to Successor Trustee together. The first thing they found they needed to do was to get several certified copies of Jack's certificate of death.

They next proceeded to remove Jack's name as co-trustee of their Living Trust on all assets that had formal legal title. Jill and Joan reviewed the Schedule of Assets and Location Index and were able to find all of the family's important documents in a matter of minutes. They found that the following assets were in the Living Trust: (1) the home; (2) the stocks and bonds; (3) the savings account; and (4) the proceeds of Jack's life insurance policy.

Jill wrote to Jack's life insurance company, sending it a certificate of death and instruction letter to make the proceeds of the policy payable to Jill, as the sole remaining trustee of the Living Trust. When the check came she made certain to deposit it in her savings account, which was inside the Living Trust, and not to her checking account, which was outside the Living Trust.

Jill proceeded to remove Jack's name as co-trustee of the Living Trust on the stocks and bonds and the savings account by sending the brokerage firm and the bank copies of Jack's certificate of death and simple instruction letters as set forth in the Instructions to Successor Trustee.

Jill went to the attorney who had prepared her Living Trust to have Jack's name removed from the deed to their home. The attorney's fee for preparing the documents necessary to make the transfer was $125.

Since all of these assets were in the Living Trust, no probate was required. But what about the assets they had left

How Will My Complete Estate Plan Work in Life and Death Situations?

out of the Living Trust? When Jill and Joan checked the Schedule of Assets, they found that the following assets had not been transferred to the Living Trust: (1) the two cars; (2) the checking account; and (3) Jack's IRA.

The checking account and the two cars were all in joint tenancy, just as their attorney had advised. Taking Jack's name off title was a simple matter of sending the DMV and the bank certificates of death and simple instruction letters. Since Jill was named as the beneficiary of Jack's IRA, all she needed to do was write to the mutual fund where Jack had invested his retirement money, again including a certificate of death and a simple instruction letter. Jill decided to liquidate the mutual fund and deposited the cash proceeds in her savings account. Since this accounted for all of their assets, Jack's Pour Over Will was never needed, just as they planned.

When Jack and Jill first established their Complete Estate Plan five years ago, their gross estate was worth $1,200,000 and their net estate was worth $1,000,000. Jill had been watching the monthly statements from the brokerage firm for their stocks and bonds and the statements from the mutual fund on Jack's IRA and knew that their investments had increased in value over the last five years. She also knew that real

estate in her neighborhood had continued to appreciate substantially, as it had for the past several years.

After reviewing the instructions from her attorney, Jill knew it was important to establish values of any appreciated property at the time of Jack's death. The brokerage account statements were sufficient for the stocks and bonds, but an appraisal was necessary for the home.

After reviewing all current figures, Jill and Joan were able to determine that Jack and Jill's gross estate at the time of Jack's death had increased from $1,200,000 to $1,400,000 and their net estate had increased from $1,000,000 to $1,200,000.

Jill and Joan were able to complete the entire transfer process in a matter of several days instead of the one to two years it would have taken through probate process. Minimum statutory probate fees on Jack's one-half of the couple's gross estate of $1,400,000 would have been $30,300. Jill paid no probate fees at all. Jill also paid no estate taxes at all, but she wouldn't even if she hadn't planned her estate because of the unlimited marital deduction for spouses.

Since Jill had an A-B Trust, she now for the first time had to divide her assets into the A Trust (the surviving spouse's trust) and the B Trust (the deceased spouse's trust). Joan had her ac-

Chapter 9

How Will My Complete Estate Plan Work in Life and Death Situations?

countant allocate the net assets as follows: $600,000 into the A Trust and $600,000 into the B Trust. At the point of Jack's death the B Trust became irrevocable. This means that Jill could no longer either modify or revoke the B Trust. As a practical matter, this means that even if Jill got angry at her children, she could not disinherit them from anything in the B Trust at her death. This was Jack's half of the joint property. He wanted his half of the estate to go to his wife first and then to his children. Jill is not allowed to change that provision.

The A Trust, however, remains revocable, which means that at any time during her lifetime, Jill may change or even eliminate the A Trust. If she remarries, she may leave the proceeds of the A Trust to her new husband and not to her children. She is just as free to deal with the A Trust as she and Jack were to deal with the entire Living Trust prior to Jack's death.

Since the B Trust is now irrevocable, Jill must keep two sets of records and file two separate income tax returns. One return, on the usual Form 1040, is in her own name, under her own social security number. The second return is a special trust income tax return on Form 1041 in the name of the trust, with a special tax identification number that

Jill's accountant obtained for her. This procedure had to be followed in all years subsequent to Jack's death. In the year Jack died, however, Jill was allowed to file one last joint income tax return on Form 1040 just as she and Jack had done previously. Jill did not have to file a Form 706 estate tax return within nine months of Jack's death because his net estate was not more than $600,000.

As we will see later, Jill exercised her right to take all of the income from the B Trust each year, so the B Trust never ended up with any taxable income. The Form 1041 was merely an informational return, showing the income transferred from the B Trust to Jill, who, of course, had to pay taxes on the income on her own return. If the B Trust had accumulated any income, it would have had to pay the tax instead of Jill.

Does this mean that Jill is now cut off from using the assets in the B Trust as she was able to do prior to Jack's death? The answer is, yes and no (always a good answer for a lawyer). Under the law, Jill is entitled to take all of the income from any assets in the B Trust for herself. In addition, Jill is entitled to sell any asset in the B Trust as long as she keeps the proceeds of the sale in the B Trust (remember, as trustee, she has the right to manage the assets of the trust). But if Jill needs any of the assets in the

How Will My Complete Estate Plan Work in Life and Death Situations?

B Trust to maintain her lifestyle as it was prior to Jack's death and her other assets (the A Trust) are not sufficient, or impractical to use for income (such as the residence) she may also use the assets of the B Trust or sell them and use the proceeds for herself in order to maintain that lifestyle or to provide for her medical needs. In addition, the law allows Jill to take either 5% of the B Trust assets or $5,000, whichever is greater, each year, whether she needs it or not. If Jack didn't want her to have these rights, he could have prevented her from doing so when their Living Trust was written, but Jack wanted Jill to have the widest possible latitude in dealing with their assets, so he allowed her these rights as well (actually, it was reciprocal, because when the Living Trust was written, neither spouse knew who was going to be the first to die and who was going to be in the shoes of the surviving spouse having to deal with an irrevocable B Trust).

We generally recommend against including the 5% or $5,000 invasion provision because it allows the entire B Trust to be taken by the surviving spouse in twenty years or less.

As a practical matter, Jill is pretty much able to continue managing her affairs as she was prior to Jack's death. She just has to have her accountant pre-pare an extra tax return each year (both state and federal) and remember not to take the principal of the B Trust for herself unless the assets in the A Trust are exhausted and she needs it for her health, maintenance or support.

Shortly after Jack's death, Jill decided that she no longer needed the big house. Jack was gone. Joan was married, and Jim was away at college. She decided to sell the house and buy a much smaller condo. Jill realized how lucky she was. The real estate market in her neighborhood was good right now. If Jack's estate had been tied up in probate, there's no telling how much red tape and delay would have been involved. She might have had to wait months and lost the peak of the market. This way she was free to choose the time and terms of the sale.

But what about taxes on the sale of the house? Jack and Jill had paid $150,000 for the house several years ago, but they lived in the San Francisco Bay Area, and the hot residential real estate market allowed Jill to sell the house for a net of $600,000, a gain of $450,000. Jill intended to "buy-down." That is, the condo she wanted was far less expensive than the house she sold, so she couldn't take advantage of rolling her profit over to the next residence. Also, Jill was only 52 years old, so she couldn't

How Will My Complete Estate Plan Work in Life and Death Situations?

even take advantage of the once-in-a-lifetime $125,000 exemption to reduce her taxable gain. But because she and Jack had taken the house out of joint tenancy and converted it to community property inside their Living Trust, Jill had received a full step-up in basis. This meant that the basis of the house was its value on the date of Jack's death. Since Jill sold the house shortly after Jack died, there was no taxable gain on the sale of the residence at all. The death income tax on the sale of the residence was entirely eliminated. Jill's $125,000 once-in-a-lifetime exemption was also preserved to be used if she ever sold the condo at a gain.

Jill had placed her $600,000 residence in the A Trust to keep the $125,000 exemption for herself and the investments and other assets worth $600,000 in the B Trust. Jill found that with the non-taxed gain she made from the sale of the house, she was quite comfortable without having to look to the B Trust for income, so she switched her investment objectives from income to growth. With the step-up in basis on the stocks and bonds at Jack's death there was no problem in liquidating the old portfolio. Without the step-up in basis there would have been a taxable gain of $100,000 on the sale of their old investments.

Jill turned out to be a shrewd investor.

Over the next five years the growth stocks in the B Trust increased in value from $600,000 to $900,000.

The value of the A Trust remained relatively stable at $600,000. Jill was living comfortably from the income from the gain she had made from the sale of her house.

Unfortunately, five years after Jack's untimely death from head injuries, history repeated itself and Jill's car also tumbled down the same hill that had taken Jack's life. Jill was spared Jack's fate on the respirator and died instantly.

Joan, of course, knew exactly what to do. She had helped Jill to settle Jack's affairs after his death five years ago, and Jill had continued to keep Joan informed on the status of the working book and any changes in plans or assets. Joan was able to quickly carry out Jill's wish to make an anatomical gift, which saved a young girl's life, and then carry out Jill's funeral and burial instructions.

Jill had retained all of her assets in the Living Trust, so Jill's Pour Over Will was never used, just as planned. Joan was able to settle Jill's estate with no probate just by changing the name of the trustee of the Living Trust from Jill to herself in the same manner as she had with her father's estate.

Joan started to become concerned about estate taxes. She knew that they

How Will My Complete Estate Plan Work in Life and Death Situations?

were due nine months after Jill's death. Joan remembered that the purpose of Jack and Jill's A-B Trust was to shelter $1,200,000 from estate taxes, but because of Jill's successful investment program, her estate had increased to $1,500,000 ($600,000 in the A Trust and $900,000 in the B Trust). Jill had also eliminated all debts and the net estate and gross estate now both had the same value. Joan was happy that she had saved so much in probate fees and on estate taxes on the first $1,200,000 in Joan's estate that she was almost happy to pay the estate taxes on the next $300,000 in the estate.

When Joan brought her figures to her tax accountant she was delighted to find that there was no estate tax on the A Trust because of Jill's $600,000 exemption (which she already knew), but also there was no estate tax on the B Trust because it was already taxed at Jack's death (with no taxes actually paid because of Jack's $600,000 exemption). The B Trust would not be subject to estate taxes again no matter what the value of its assets had become by the time of Jill's death. Joan's accountant did not have to file a Form 706 estate tax return within nine months of Jill's death because the value of the A Trust did not exceed $600,000.

It should be noted that although there were no estate taxes on the apprecia-

tion of assets in the B Trust on Jill's death, there will be capital gains taxes on the appreciation from $600,000 to $900,000 when the assets are eventually sold.

With the entire estate of $1,500,000 intact, Joan proceeded to carry out the terms of the Living Trust. Jill had never changed the distribution provisions of the A Trust, so both Jack and Jill's trusts were to be distributed equally to Joan and Jim, with distribution of the principal delayed to age 30 in each case.

Since Joan was now 33 and Jim was 27, Joan, as successor trustee of the Living Trust, distributed one-half of the estate to herself free of the Living Trust. She retained the balance in the Living Trust, paying all the income from the Living Trust to Jim over the next three years. Jim had a medical emergency one year, so Joan also distributed a small portion of the principal of the Living Trust to Jim that year to cover his medical expenses.

When Jim reached 30 years of age, Joan distributed all of the principal to him and closed the Living Trust. It had done its job. It had avoided probate on both Jack and Jill's estate; it avoided a conservatorship when Jack was incapacitated; it avoided death income taxes when Jill sold the family home and liquidated their old investment program and it avoided

135

How Will My Complete Estate Plan Work in Life and Death Situations?

estate taxes on Jill's death. Let's hope that Joan and Jim learned well from their parents and have established their own Living Trusts.

Let's take a look at the Hill family's financial savings for a moment. It's easier to focus on than their emotional savings, because numbers are involved. But just because it's easier, let's never forget the emotional drain saved by the elimination of the conservatorship and the two probates.

For purposes of our financial analysis, let's be conservative and assume that only statutory probate fees would have been charged. Let's also assume an income tax rate of 28%. The actual rate for some people goes as high as 33% for a portion of their income, but we'll ignore that for simplicity and to determine a conservative estimate of the Hill family savings.

Conservatorship. When Jack became incapacitated, no conservatorship proceedings were necessary. Unlike probate, there are no statutory fees for conservatorships. Since Jack's incapacity was brief and the matters handled while he was incapacitated were few and simple, let's assume a savings of $2,500. Obviously, it could have been much higher.

Had Jack been allowed to linger, brain dead, on the respirator much longer, there could have been a devastating financial as well as emotional impact on the Hill family. Jack's Durable Power of Attorney for Health Care Services solved that problem before it began. Since there is no way to measure these savings, they won't be included in our analysis.

Jack's Probate. When Jack died, Jack and Jill's gross estate was worth $1,400,000. Since this was all community property, Jack's gross estate was valued at $700,000. Statutory probate fees would have been $30,300.

Death Income Taxes on Sale of Home. The original basis of the home was $150,000 and it was sold for a net of $600,000, a $450,000 gain. Had Jack and Jill continued to hold the house in joint tenancy, only half of the value of the residence would have been stepped-up on Jack's death. With a joint tenancy the basis would have been increased from $150,000 to $375,000 (Jack's $75,000 basis is stepped up to $300,000, but Jill's basis stays at $75,000 for a total of $375,000), for a taxable gain of $225,000. At 28% that's $63,000 in federal death income taxes on the sale of the home. Add more for state death income taxes.

Also, remember when the home was

How Will My Complete Estate Plan Work in Life and Death Situations?

sold, Jill was able to act right away. She was not caught in the delays caused by probate. By maintaining control of her assets, Jill was able to get top dollar for her house. But since there's really no way to measure this, we won't include this savings in our analysis.

Death Income Taxes on Sale of Investments. Jill had a $100,00 gain on the sale of her investment portfolio. Had the portfolio remained in joint tenancy there would have been a taxable gain of $50,000, resulting in $14,000 of death income taxes.

Note here that to the extent you choose to probate joint tenancy property to set aside the joint tenancy, you can also avoid these death income taxes. To the extent you don't probate the assets, you will reduce your probate fees. Only the Living Trust will both avoid probate and avoid death income taxes at the same time, but you won't be subject to both probate fees and death income taxes on the same items of property, even without a Living Trust.

Jill's Probate. When Jill died her gross estate was worth $1,500,000. Statutory probate fees on a gross estate of $1,500,000 are $52,300. Arbitrarily, let's reduce Jill's gross estate by $100,000. This should cover the loss she would have

suffered through either probate or death income taxes on Jack's death and also conservatorship costs on Jack's incapacity. Statutory probate fees on a gross estate of $1,400,000 are $50,300.

Estate Taxes. Again, to be conservative, let's assume a net estate of $1,300,000 instead of $1,500,000. The $200,000 difference should cover deductions for both probates and for death income taxes. Without estate planning, only $600,000 would be exempt, leaving $700,000 to be subjected to estate taxes. The Hill family would have paid $276,500 in estate taxes on Jill's death if she and Jack had not established their A-B Living Trust.

Since the probate costs of eliminating joint tenancies ($30,300 if we don't count extraordinary fees) is lower than the death income taxes on the sale of the home and investment portfolio ($63,000 for the home and $14,000 for the portfolio), we'll assume that if Jack and Jill did not have a Living Trust Jill would have probated these assets when Jack died and petitioned the court to set aside the joint tenancies. This would have left her with probate costs of $30,300 on Jack's death and no death income taxes on the sale of the home and the portfolio.

We know that many of you are thinking that you're not the Hill family.

How Will My Complete Estate Plan Work in Life and Death Situations?

Hill Family Estate Planning Savings

Conservatorship	$ 2,500
Jack's Probate	30,300
Jill's Probate	50,300
Estate Taxes	<u>276,500</u>
Gross Savings	$ 359,600
Cost of Establishing Living Trust	<u>- 900</u>
Net Savings	$ 358,700

How Will My Complete Estate Plan Work in Life and Death Situations?

You're single. Or your estate isn't as large as the Hill family's. Or your estate isn't as small as the Hill family's. Or your life just doesn't fit into the perfect pattern of the Hill family that we chose for our example.

You're right. We chose the Hill family as an example to show you how the Complete Estate Plan is intended to work in life and death situations. While we tried to be conservative in analyzing the financial benefits of proper estate planning, we did pick an ideal family for our demonstration.

Life is not perfect, and you probably don't fit in exactly the same pattern as the Hill family (if you do, we would advise you not to drive on the infamous hill that both Jack and Jill had trouble with).

Remember though, no matter what your situation is, you _do_ have an estate plan. You can either accept the government's estate plan, with maximum fees, taxes, delays and loss of privacy, or you can take your life into your own hands and create an estate plan that fits your needs, that puts you and your family in control of your estate, that minimizes or eliminates delays, loss of privacy, fees and taxes and that gives you the peace of mind in knowing that you've given yourself and your family one of the best of all possible gifts.

Chapter 10

More Questions and More Answers

Q. How large should my estate be before I need a Living Trust?

A. All gross estates over $60,000 are subject to probate. A gross estate of $100,000 is subject to over $6,000 in probate costs and is definitely a candidate for a Living Trust.

Q. Can I be the trustor, trustee and beneficiary of my own Living Trust?

A. Yes, provided you name a successor trustee and successor beneficiary.

Q. Does my spouse have to be the co-trustee of my Living Trust?

A. No. It's customary for your spouse to be co-trustee, but it's not required by law.

Q. Can I set up a Living Trust without an attorney?

A. Yes, but a Living Trust is a technical legal document. If you attempt to copy someone else's document, you may leave out something important for your situation or put in something inappropriate for your situation. Considering the importance of your estate plan, legal fees of attorneys specializing in setting up Living Trusts should be fairly insignificant compared to potential savings in probate fees, conservatorship fees, death income taxes and estate taxes.

Q. What are the disadvantages of a Living Trust?

A. (1) If you refinance real estate in the Living Trust, you will probably be required to take the property out of the Living Trust prior to the refinance and put it back into the Living Trust after the refinance. (2) Probate allows the claims of your creditors to be cut off unless they make claims against the estate

Chapter 10

More Questions and More Answers

within four months after the executor publishes notice of your death and assets are distributed. The Living Trust does not change any applicable statute of limitations on creditor claims. Statutes of limitations vary in length depending on the nature of the claim. (3) If you want full protection from probate, you must make certain that you take title to all appropriate assets as trustee of your Living Trust. (4) You should take funds out of your Living Trust before you make any gifts subject to the $10,000 annual exclusion. (5) If you have an A-B Trust, the surviving spouse must keep two sets of records and file two separate state and federal tax returns each year. This is also true of a testamentary trust as well as of a Living Trust. It's the price a married couple must pay to make sure both parties can take full advantage of their own $600,000 estate tax exemption and the unlimited marital deduction.

Q. If I have a Living Trust, exactly how should I take title to my assets?

A. If your Living Trust is dated March 1, 1990, take title as follows: "John Doe and Mary Doe, Trustees, U.D.T., dated March 1, 1990." "U.D.T."

means "under declaration of trust."

Q. How can I "take title" to assets like my personal effects that don't have title registered with anyone?

A. Instead of taking title to those assets, you just sign an assignment of those assets to the Living Trust and keep a copy of the assignment with your Living Trust.

Q. What assets should I keep outside my Living Trust?

A. (1) Most motor vehicles.
(2) A small checking account.
(3) Retirement plans, such as IRAs, 401(k) plans, Keogh plans, profit sharing plans and pension plans.

Q. Who should be the beneficiary of my retirement plans?

A. Whomever you want, but generally your spouse. You can name your Living Trust as contingent beneficiary.

Q. Who should be the beneficiary of my life insurance policies?

A. Name your Living Trust as the beneficiary of your life insurance policies.

Q. Do I need an Insurance Trust?

A. Generally Insurance Trusts are recommended only when the inclusion

More Questions and More Answers

of insurance death benefits in your net estate causes some or all of the insurance death benefits to be taxed. This will begin at over $600,000 for a single person and at over $1,200,000 for married couples with an A-B Trust or an A-B-C Trust.

Q. Why does the IRS require two tax returns for an A-B Trust after the death of the first spouse but not before?

A. Since your Living Trust is revocable during the joint lifetime of the parties, the IRS does not care about its existence. Once the first spouse dies the B Trust becomes irrevocable, and the IRS considers the B Trust to be one separate tax-paying entity and the surviving spouse to be another separate tax-paying entity. The surviving spouse files on Form 1040, as usual, and the B Trust files on Form 1041.

Q. With an A-B-C Trust are there three sets of records that must be kept each year after the death of the first spouse?

A. Yes.

Q. Will my real estate be reassessed if I transfer it to a Living Trust?

A. No.

Q. Will I have to pay a transfer tax to transfer my real estate to my Living Trust?

A. No. All you will have to pay is the recorder's fee for recording your grant deed. It's usually around $9 per transfer.

Q. Will I have to pay a gift tax to transfer my property to my Living Trust?

A. No. No new taxes result from the formation of a Living Trust.

Q. Do I have to get a special tax I.D. number for my Living Trust?

A. No. No special tax I.D. number is required until after the first spouse dies with either an A-B Trust or an A-B-C Trust. While both spouses are alive your income tax return will look exactly as it would have if you had not established a Living Trust.

Q. If I only own a one-half interest in a piece of real estate, can I transfer that interest into my Living Trust?

A. Yes. The grant deed making the transfer would read: "John Doe, as to an undivided one-half interest, grants to John Doe, Trustee, U.D.T., dated March 1, 1990, as to an undivided one-half interest . . ."

Chapter 10

More Questions and More Answers

Q. <u>Can a person have more than one Living Trust at a time?</u>

A. Yes. It's not customary, but it is possible. For example, a wife with separate property could set up her own Living Trust for just that separate property. She and her husband could then set up a joint Living Trust for their community property. The Living Trust is extremely flexible and can take many forms. That's one reason it's dangerous to just copy another person's documents. They may not be the right documents for your situation.

Q. <u>What is separate property?</u>

A. Generally it's property you owned prior to your marriage, property you inherited and property that was given to you that you have not co-mingled with your spouse's separate or community property and the income from that property.

Q. <u>What is community property?</u>

A. Generally it's all property earned or acquired by either spouse during the term of the marriage except by way of gift or inheritance. If your property cannot be clearly established to be separate property, it's generally presumed to be community property.

Q. <u>What is quasi-community property?</u>

A. Generally it's property brought into the jurisdiction of a community property state (like California) that was acquired in a non-community property state (like New York) that was acquired in such a manner that it would have been community property had it been acquired in a community property state. For most purposes quasi-community property is treated just like community property in the community property state. As an example, husband and wife acquire all their property while residing in New York as a result of husband's earnings. The couple later moves to California to take up permanent residence and brings all their property with them. Their property is quasi-community property and will be treated just like community property under California law for most purposes.

Q. <u>What practical difference does it make whether my property is separate, community or quasi-community?</u>

A. In a divorce you're entitled to all your separate property and one-half of your community and quasi-community property. At your death you have the power to dispose of all of your separate property and one-half of your community and quasi-community property. When you die, there is a 100% step-up in basis on your separate property, your community property and your quasi-community property. On your spouse's death there is a 100% step-up in basis on your community property and on your quasi-community property but there is no step-up in basis at all on your separate property.

Q. What is basis?

A. Generally it's what something originally cost. Basis is then adjusted by certain factors (such as the cost of certain improvements on real estate), to determine the taxable gain when the property is sold. The gain is the sales price, adjusted by certain factors, less the adjusted basis.

Q. What is stepped-up basis?

A. Upon the death of the owner of property, the property gets a new basis. That owner's interest in the property is given a new basis equal to the value of that property on the date of death. The increase in value, if any, is never taxed. This is not a tax deferral. It's total tax escape. The amount of the step up in basis de-

pends on how title to the property is held on the date of death.

Q. Why does community property get a 100% step-up in basis and joint tenancy property only a 50% step-up in basis?

A. The people who wrote the tax codes take the position that joint tenancy property is divisible into two parts, each of which can be treated separately, but that community property is a unity that has to be treated as a whole. Since it's really a bonus to get the 100% step-up in basis on community property, we shouldn't argue with the rules even if they don't make sense — just try to take advantage of any legitimate tax break that we can.

Q. What can be done with joint tenancy property to get the 100% step-up in basis?

A. There are three solutions. (1) Convert the joint tenancy property to community property during your lifetime. You will receive the 100% step-up in basis, but the property will be subject to probate. (2) Let your executor worry about it. Your executor can petition the Probate Court to set aside the joint tenancy

Chapter 10

More Questions and More Answers

and probate the property to receive the 100% step-up in basis. This is costly and time-consuming. (3) Put the property into a Living Trust and convert it to community property. This is the best solution because you get the 100% step-up in basis and avoid probate at the same time.

Q. Do single people have to worry about the step-up in basis?

A. Generally the answer is no. Unless you are recently divorced and all your property affairs are not yet settled, single people cannot have community property. The step-up in basis is still applicable to you, but there is no special planning you need do because you can't convert your property to community property.

Q. Is the Living Trust a new idea?

A. No. The Living Trust traces its origins back to at least medieval England and, perhaps, to even more ancient Roman law. It has been used in this country for years by wealthy families with highly paid, sophisticated attorneys to avoid probate, avoid conservatorship, eliminate or minimize death income taxes, eliminate or minimize estate taxes and preserve privacy. Notable famous examples are John F. Kennedy and

Bing Crosby. What is new is the realization that the Living Trust is not just for the super-wealthy. It works for almost everyone. Moreover, attorneys who specialize in preparing Living Trusts can now make them affordable for almost everyone.

Q. What is the cost of obtaining a Living Trust?

A. Costs vary from law office to law office. Usually attorneys who specialize in preparing the Living Trust can do the job better, faster and less expensively than non-specialists. Specialists will usually quote you a fixed fee rather than an hourly rate once they know what you want and need in conjunction with your Living Trust.

Q. Are all Living Trusts pretty much the same?

A. No. There is no "standard form" for a Living Trust. Each attorney has his or her own format which must be adapted to the special needs of each client.

Q. How long does it take to establish a Living Trust?

A. In an emergency, by pulling out all stops, it can be done in a day or two. But under normal circumstances, count on between two to three weeks between when you first see your attorney and when you finally sign the documents. You also need to add in the time it takes you to prepare for the first meeting with the attorney and the time it will take after the documents are signed to transfer your property to the Living Trust. The total process is usually four to five weeks after you make the decision to go forward.

Q. <u>The Living Trust sounds too good to be true. Won't Congress try to abolish it?</u>

A. No one can predict Congress, of course, but we don't think so. You can break the financial advantages of the Living Trust into two groups: (1) avoidance of probate and avoidance of conservatorship; and (2) elimination of death income taxes and elimination or minimization of estate taxes. Congress has no interest at all in probate and conservatorship avoidance. Probate fees and conservatorship fees are not taxes. They are not revenue generating proceedings for the government. Death income taxes and inheritance taxes, the second group, are, of course, of vital government concern. However, there is no move in Congress to challenge the testamentary trust, which is well established in the tax codes to handle estate taxes. There is also no move in Congress to change the basis rules for community property. There is nothing the Living Trust does that Congress is concerned about that can't be done by other means. The unique aspect of the Living Trust, of course, is that it solves your probate and conservatorship problems at the same time it's solving your tax problems. Remember, politicians are people too and these tax advantages help their families. We consider it interesting to note that the average net worth of our Congressperson is $1,000,000 and that the federal estate tax exemption for a married couple is $1,200,000.

Q. <u>Will my property receive a step-up in basis when I transfer it to my Living Trust?</u>

A. No. The step-up in basis occurs after the death of the person who transferred it to the Living Trust.

Q. <u>Is there another step-up in basis after the second spouse dies?</u>

A. Yes. There is a step-up in basis for the assets in the A Trust, but not for the assets in the B or the C Trusts.

Chapter 10

More Questions and More Answers

Q. How do I establish the value of an asset at the date of death for purposes of establishing a new basis?

A. An appraisal for real estate and any other asset where values are not regularly quoted and brokerage account statements for stocks, bonds and other securities.

Q. If I already have a Living Trust, how often should it be reviewed?

A. We recommend you review it yourself annually to make certain it still fits your needs and to make certain all of your assets are in the Living Trust. Congress passed a law on September 11, 1981 that made a major change in estate tax law. All estate planning documents (wills, testamentary trusts and Living Trusts) written prior to September 11, 1981 should be reviewed and updated by your attorney.

Q. What government agency regulates Living Trusts?

A. None. No government agency regulates wills, testamentary trusts or Living Trusts.

Q. Where do I record my Living Trust?

A. You don't have to record your Liv-ing Trust. It's a private document. You may have to show it to those you are doing business with, however. For example, if you are borrowing money from a bank, the bank will usually ask to see all or part of the declaration of trust to make sure the trustee has the power to borrow. All well written Living Trusts give the trustees the power to do anything with the assets in the Living Trust the trustors could have done before the assets were put in the Living Trust.

Q. Will I lose any income tax deductions by putting my assets in the Living Trust?

A. No.

Q. Is a Living Trust a tax shelter?

A. No, not in the way people usually refer to a tax shelter. While both spouses are alive, there are no income tax advantages or disadvantages to the Living Trust. The Living Trust will minimize or eliminate estate taxes and death income taxes for married couples after death, but not ordinary income taxes.

Q. Will putting my assets in a Living Trust protect them against my creditors?

A. No. The purpose of a Living Trust is to avoid probate, to avoid conservatorship, to eliminate death income taxes, to eliminate or minimize estate taxes and to promote privacy. It is not a device to protect your assets from your creditors.

Q. How can I protect my assets from my creditors?

A. That's beyond the scope of this book, but some attorneys do recommend a special type of Living Trust as a means of protecting your assets from creditors. The standard estate planning Living Trust will neither help nor hinder you in dealing with your creditors, however.

Q. Can I pledge my Living Trust to creditors to secure a loan?

A. No, you don't pledge your Living Trust. Instead you, as trustee, can pledge any and all assets in the Living Trust to secure a loan, just as you could have done if there were no Living Trust.

Q. What is the Rule Against Perpetuities?

A. It's an ancient doctrine in the law to prohibit any trust, including a Living Trust, from lasting into perpetuity. The Rule says all trusts must terminate within the lifetime of the last person mentioned in the trust to die plus twenty-one years. Since most Living Trusts are meant to terminate within the lifetime of people specifically named in the Living Trust, there is usually no practical problem with the Rule Against Perpetuities.

Q. Is there any advantage of valuing my assets when I put them in my Living Trust?

A. No.

Q. Is it possible for one spouse to have a Living Trust and not the other?

A. Yes, but it won't work as well for you. The spouse with the Living Trust will only be able to deal with his or her separate property and half of the couple's community property.

Q. Why would a single person want to have a Living Trust?

A. To avoid probate and to avoid conservatorship. A Living Trust will not help a single person with death income taxes or estate taxes. One or more of the other trusts mentioned in this book may be helpful to single people, however.

Q. Who should a single person select

Chapter 10

More Questions and More Answers

<u>as a successor trustee</u>?

A. Someone you trust. The same person you would pick to be the executor of your estate or you would pick to take care of your affairs if you were incapacitated.

Q. <u>What happens to my Living Trust if I get divorced</u>?

A. The joint Living Trust should be revoked and each party should set up his or her own Living Trust with the assets obtained out of the divorce.

Q. <u>Will having a Living Trust help or hurt in a divorce situation</u>?

A. Neither. A Living Trust will not help or hinder you in a divorce; however, the way you have listed your property as community or separate in your Living Trust documents will at the most be conclusive and at the least be highly presumptive that that's how the property should be characterized in the divorce.

Q. <u>Can two single people living together have a single Living Trust as married couples do</u>?

A. Yes. As a matter of fact, two single people who aren't even living together can create a joint Living Trust. The only thing they can't do

is to change their separate property to community property. The law reserves community property status to married couples.

Q. <u>If I sign a new will after I've created my Living Trust, will it revoke my Living Trust</u>?

A. No, but it will probably revoke your Pour Over Will. If you've placed all of your assets in your Living Trust, your new will will be ineffective. If you want to revoke your Living Trust for some reason, you should sign a statement saying that you're revoking the Living Trust and transfer title to all assets in the Living Trust back to yourself as an individual.

Q. <u>If I have a Living Trust, why do I need a will</u>?

A. You don't need an ordinary will; you need a Pour Over Will. The purpose of a Pour Over Will is to make certain assets you've forgotten to put into the Living Trust during your lifetime at least get there after your death. The Pour Over Will is also an appropriate place to designate the guardian of your minor children or incapacitated adult children.

Q. <u>Will a will control the disposition</u>

of property I hold in joint tenancy?

A. No. No matter what you say in your will, the property you hold in joint tenancy will go to the joint tenant at your death. However, there is a procedure to set aside the joint tenancy and probate the asset if all interested parties are in agreement. This is expensive and time consuming.

Q. Will a will control who gets my life insurance benefits?

A. No, unless you've named your estate as beneficiary.

Q. Will a will control who gets my retirement plan benefits after my death?

A. Not unless you've named your estate as the beneficiary.

Q. Will a will control who gets the property in my Living Trust?

A. No. The Living Trust document will control how assets inside the Living Trust are distributed after your death.

Q. What is an unfunded Living Trust?

A. A Living Trust with no assets in it. Under English and American common law there could be no trust without "trust res" (also called a "trust corpus"), which in English means

without some property in it. There is statutory law changing this for Living Trusts, and some attorneys do create unfunded Living Trusts. We do not recommend this for you. We recommend that you put at least one asset, no matter how little value it may have, into your Living Trust on the day you sign your Living Trust documents. Further, we recommend that you transfer the rest of your assets into the Living Trust as soon thereafter as practical.

Q. Is there such a thing as an irrevocable Living Trust?

A. Yes and no. In this book we've reserved the title "Living Trust" with a capital "L" and a capital "T" for revocable living trusts, but there certainly are irrevocable living trusts with a little "l" and a little "t." The Insurance Trust and the Children's Trust we've mentioned in this book are irrevocable living trusts. They're living trusts (and not testamentary trusts) because they are effective during your lifetime.

Q. What are the annual fees for a Living Trust?

A. None. However, most Living Trust documents do provide for a fee for the successor trustee.

Chapter 10

More Questions and More Answers

Q. Who keeps a record of the assets in the Living Trust?

A. You do. You don't have to notify your attorney or anyone else that you're buying or selling assets in the Living Trust. A Living Trust is meant to keep you in charge of your own life.

Q. Can parents create a Living Trust with their children?

A. Yes. The Living Trust is an extremely flexible form of property ownership. However, just because something is possible doesn't mean it's desirable. In most cases it's fine to have one or more children as successor trustee but not as co-trustee.

Q. What's the difference between a co-trustee and a successor trustee?

A. A successor trustee only gains power if both co-trustees are either dead or incapacitated. A co-trustee has equal power with you while you are still alive and have full capacity and and then has full power after your death and incapacity. Most people, but not all people, will only want a spouse as co-trustee, just as most people prefer one or more adult children as successor trustee.

Q. Who should be my successor trustee if my children don't get along with each other?

A. A Living Trust will not help nor will it hurt this situation. You can't force your children to get along with each other, but you can try to minimize the potential for conflict. Make sure your directions as to the disposition of your personal property are absolutely clear and cover all your personal effects. Warring siblings will find any excuse to be angry with one another. You might want to consider an independent successor trustee in this situation.

Q. Can a Living Trust be challenged in court like a will?

A. Yes. One of the unfortunate lessons of modern life is that anything can be challenged in court. However, we see no reason why a properly drawn Living Trust would be any more subject to attack than a will.

Q. What would be the reasons for attacking a Living Trust in court?

A. Basically they would be the same reasons that your will would be subject to attack. Usually the attack would come from someone who inherited less than he or she thought right and would either allege you lacked the proper capacity to know what you were doing or that someone was exercising undue influence over you when you signed your Living Trust.

Q. Can our Living Trust provide for children we don't have yet?

A. Absolutely. Many Living Trusts provide that after the death of both spouses the property will be equally divided among all children then living, even though those children weren't conceived at the time the Living Trust was executed.

Q. What happens if one of the beneficiaries of our Living Trust should die before we do?

A. Your Living Trust should take that contingency into account. You normally either divide the deceased beneficiary's portion among the remaining beneficiaries or give the deceased beneficiary's portion to his or her children. When a child predeceases the parent, most parents prefer to leave the deceased child's portion to the deceased child's children and not to the deceased child's spouse. But this is a matter of personal preference. You can do anything you want.

Q. What do I have to do to disinherit a child?

A. Your Pour Over Will should mention the names of all your children and indicate those who you are disinheriting. The law takes the position that your failure to mention a natural object of your bounty may mean that you've forgotten them rather than intentionally omitted them and give them a right to challenge the will and the Living Trust. It is not necessary to give them one dollar. We consider it wise to handwrite a note and send it to your attorney stating why you are disinheriting a child.

Q. How old do you have to be to have a Living Trust?

A. Generally you must be at least eighteen years of age to be either a trustor, trustee, co-trustee or successor trustee of a Living Trust. Whether you should have a Living Trust is not contingent on your age, but rather on the size of your estate.

Q. I had an A-B Living Trust with my first spouse who passed away. Can I form a new Living Trust with my second spouse?

A. Yes, but the only assets you can contribute to the second Living Trust

Chapter 10

More Questions and More Answers

are those in your A Trust. The B Trust with your first spouse is now irrevocable and cannot be included in your second Living Trust.

Q. <u>When are estate taxes payable?</u>
A. Nine months after death.

Q. <u>What kind of tax return has to be filed for estate taxes?</u>
A. A Form 706 Federal Estate Tax Return must be filed within nine months of a death if your estate is more than $600,000. Remember, if you are married and if you and your spouse have a combined estate of $1,000,000, then upon the death of the first of you no estate tax return has to be filed as the interest of the first to die is only $500,000.

Q. <u>What kind of tax return has to be filed for death income taxes?</u>
A. The usual Form 1040. Death income taxes are just a form of capital gains tax (currently charged at the same rate as for ordinary income) that are reportable and taxable at the same time and manner as any other capital gains tax.

Q. <u>Does having a Living Trust increase my chances of a tax audit?</u>
A. No. During your lifetime the IRS is

not even aware that you have a Living Trust. After the death of the first spouse, the IRS treats a Living Trust just as it does testamentary trust. The IRS doesn't care whether your trust is a Living Trust or a testamentary trust.

Q. <u>Can my successor trustee make any changes to my Living Trust?</u>
A. No. Only the trustor (you), or if more than one, the co-trustors (usually you and your spouse) acting together can change your Living Trust.

Q. <u>What if my co-trustor and I have a disagreement about our Living Trust?</u>
A. Unless both of you can agree on a change in the Living Trust, it will remain the same as when you originally signed it or last agreed on an amendment. Either co-trustor, however, can revoke the entire Living Trust at any time without the consent of the other co-trustor.

Q. <u>If I replace my old will with a Living Trust, do I have to notify my old attorney or destroy my old will?</u>
A. No, but it's not a bad idea to destroy all old wills to avoid any confusion.

Q. <u>Is the Living Trust recognized in</u>

all 50 states?

A. Yes.

Q. Can out of state real property be placed in a Living Trust?

A. Yes. It is not necessary to have separate Living Trusts for out of state real property. But you will have to comply with the other state's laws for transfer of your out of state real property to your Living Trust, so it is usually necessary to hire an attorney in that state to make sure the transfer is legal and proper. Personal property located out of state usually poses no special problems.

Q. Does it make a difference if my spouse or I are not U.S. citizens?

A. Yes. In 1988 Congress dramatically increased both estate and gift taxes applicable to nonresident aliens and U.S. taxpayers whose spouses are not U.S. citizens, whether or not they are resident in the U.S. If you or your spouse are not U.S. citizens and have not revised your estate plans since the 1988 amendment of the law, you should do so right away. If you or your spouse are not U.S. citizens and you have not yet made your estate plans, make sure you inform your attorney of that fact. In most cases your attorney will recommend the formation of what is called a "qualified domestic trust" or a "QDOT" which allows a tax deferral but not outright avoidance. This will be part of your Living Trust. Also, gifts to non-citizen spouses are subject to a much higher gift tax exclusion ($100,000 per year instead of $10,000) so a gifting program may be a useful part of the estate plan in this situation.

Q. What is a community property set aside?

A. It's a simpler and less expensive alternative to the usual probate procedure. It only works for married couples leaving their estates to their spouses and only on the death of the first spouse to die. Unless you have a Living Trust, the second death will trigger the full probate procedure.

Q. I've heard probate fees quoted at half of those stated in this book. Who's right?

A. The statutory fees quoted in this book are the combined fees of the executor and the attorney. The executor's fee is one-half of the rate quoted in the book, and the attorney's fee is one-half of the rate quoted in the book.

Chapter 10

More Questions and More Answers

Q. I've heard probate costs quoted at much higher amounts than those stated in this book. Who's right?

A. Total probate costs do include many items in excess of statutory fees, such as extraordinary fees, accountant's fees and appraiser's fees. But many, if not all, of these fees and costs will still be necessary whether or not there is a probate. We've tried to be conservative in this book in quoting the kind of savings you can achieve with a Living Trust so we've only included the statutory fees as your probate cost savings.

Q. If I own my house in joint tenancy with my adult child, can he or she move in without my permission?

A. Yes. The joint tenant is a co-owner and has as much legal right to occupy the property as you do.

Q. Can my joint tenant sell his or her interest in the property without my permission?

A. Yes.

Q. Can my joint tenant's creditors attach the property I own with him or her?

A. Yes.

Q. Why do you say that joint tenancy only avoids the first probate?

A. Most joint tenancies are between husband and wife. It's the form of joint tenancy that works best. When the first spouse dies, probate is avoided, but when the second spouse dies, his or her estate must still be probated unless a new joint tenancy is formed. Joint tenancies with anyone other than a spouse are usually less satisfactory. A Living Trust avoids probate on the death of both spouses without having to give someone else a present interest in your property.

Q. Will a Living Trust affect my social security benefits?

A. No.

Q. If I transfer my home to my Living Trust, will it affect my home mortgage deduction?

A. No.

Q. How do I transfer stocks and bonds that are held in street name to my Living Trust?

A. Just have the name of the brokerage account changed from yours to the Living Trust.

More Questions and More Answers

Q. <u>Will a transfer of my home to my Living Trust trigger a call on my mortgage?</u>

A. No. Since you have maintained complete control over the property the transfer is not a sale triggering the "due on sale" clause in the mortgage of your note and deed of trust. However, some mortgage companies have a clause in the mortgage requiring that they be notified in writing if you assign your interest in the property.

Q. <u>Will placing my home in my Living Trust have any effect on my $125,000 capital gains tax exemption?</u>

A. No, but after the death of the first spouse, the home should be placed in the A Trust and not the B Trust if the exemption has not been previously used. If the home is placed in the B Trust, the exemption will be lost.

Q. <u>What's a holographic will?</u>

A. A will written on plain paper, in your own handwriting, dated and signed at the bottom. It doesn't have to be witnessed and it is legal in California.

Q. <u>Doesn't the fact that I have a will</u> mean that I will avoid probate?

A. Read this book again. You didn't understand it. Seriously, it is unfortunately true that a large number of people do not understand the basic principle that a will is designed to cause probate, not to avoid it.

Q. <u>If I fill all three roles of trustor, trustee and beneficiary of my Living Trust, isn't it just a sham?</u>

A. No. No more so than you being the sole shareholder, officer and director of your corporation. You are doing something the law specifically allows you to do. The law allows you to change form without changing substance. You must name a successor trustee to act when you can't and a successor beneficiary to receive the assets in the Living Trust when you die.

Q. <u>What's a grantor trust?</u>

A. It's the name the IRS usually uses for Living Trusts.

Q. <u>What's an inter vivos trust?</u>

A. It's another name for any trust taking effect during the trustor's (maker's) lifetime. It is the opposite of a testamentary trust which only takes effect on the trustor's death. What we, and almost all other es-

Chapter 10

More Questions and More Answers

tate planners, call the Living Trust is a revocable inter vivos trust. "Inter vivos" is Latin for "during life."

Q. Doesn't a testamentary trust work as well as a Living Trust to minimize or eliminate estate taxes?

A. Yes, but it does nothing to avoid probate, to avoid conservatorship and to maintain privacy. The testamentary trust can also eliminate death income taxes, but, unlike the Living Trust, only at the cost of probating the asset.

Q. What is a Durable Power of Attorney for Health Care?

A. It's a document specifically authorized under California law (many other states have similar laws now) that you can use to appoint another person, such as a family member or friend, who can make health care decisions for you if you become unable to make those decisions on your own. The person you select may make all decisions about your health care, subject only to limitations you specify on that person's authority and several restrictions imposed by law.

Q. Why complete a Durable Power of Attorney for Health Care?

A. A Durable Power of Attorney for Health Care applies to all health care decisions and allows you to appoint a person to carry out your wishes if you become incapable of making your own decisions. The other primary reasons for completing a Durable Power of Attorney for Health Care are to avoid possible court proceedings, to avoid possible delays in receiving health care and to avoid possible stress on family or friends. The Durable Power of Attorney for Health Care is completed by filling out a form. No court proceedings are necessary. It may be advisable to execute a Durable Power of Attorney for Health Care before surgery or other medical care. Those with chronic conditions that may flare up and leave them unable to make decisions might also consider executing a Durable Power of Attorney for Health Care. As a practical matter, many people may want to keep a Durable Power of Attorney for Health Care in effect at all times, just as they maintain insurance to protect their interests in the event of unforeseen circumstances.

Q. Who can complete a Durable Power of Attorney for Health Care?

A. Any person who is a California resident, is at least 18 years old, is of sound mind and is acting on his or her own free will.

Q. Does a Durable Power of Attorney for Health Care ever have to be renewed?
A. Yes, every seven years.

Q. What is the difference between a "durable" power of attorney and a "regular" power of attorney?
A. Regular powers of attorney become void when the maker becomes incapacitated. Durable powers of attorney continue to be effective after incapacity.

Q. What is a "springing" durable power of attorney?
A. One that only becomes effective on the incapacity of the maker. It "springs" into effect when the incapacity occurs.

Q. What is a Durable General Power of Attorney?
A. A Durable General Power of Attorney applies to all non-health care decisions and allows you to appoint a person to carry out your wishes on any non-medical subject if you become incapacitated.

Q. Does a Durable General Power of Attorney also have to be renewed periodically?
A. No. That's one reason we recommend that there be two separate Durable Powers of Attorney -- one for health care and the other for all other matters. With two separate documents you avoid confusion over the effects of renewal or nonrenewal.

Q. What if I become incapacitated while my Durable Power of Attorney for Health Care is in effect but it expires before I can execute a new one?
A. If you are incapacitated, your Durable Power of Attorney for Health Care will continue in effect, even though the seven year period is exceeded, until you regain capacity. As soon as you do regain capacity, however, your previous Durable Power of Attorney for Health Care will expire and you should immediately execute a new one. If you are concerned about future incapacity (for example, you are about to undergo surgery) and your current Durable Power of Attorney for Health Care is about to expire, we advise that you execute a new one right away,

Chapter 10

More Questions and More Answers

just to be on the safe side.

Q. If I sign a Durable Power of Attorney for Health Care, does this mean I've given up any rights to make my own health care decisions while I still have the capacity to do so?

A. No. Notwithstanding your Durable Power of Attorney for Health Care, you have the right to make medical and other health care decisions for yourself so long as you can give informed consent with respect to the particular decision. In addition, no treatment may be given to you over your objection, and health care necessary to keep you alive may not be stopped if you object.

Q. What if I want to revoke my Durable Power of Attorney for Health Care?

A. You have the right to revoke the appointment of the person designated in your Durable Power of Attorney for Health Care by notifying that person of the revocation orally or in writing. You also have the right to revoke the authority of that person to make health care decisions for you by notifying your treating physician, the hospital or other health care provider orally or in writing.

Q. Will the person I appoint to make my health care decisions in my Durable Power of Attorney for Health Care be able to examine my medical records and authorize their disclosure to others?

A. Yes, unless you limit that right when you sign your Durable Power of Attorney for Health Care.

Q. Are there any restrictions on the person I select to make my health care decisions that are imposed by law that I cannot waive even if I want to?

A. Yes. By law, the person you select to make your health care decisions is not permitted to consent to any of the following: (1) commitment to or placement in a mental hospital treatment facility; (2) convulsive treatment; (3) psychosurgery; (4) sterilization; or (5) abortion.

Q. Can I exercise a "right to die" in a Durable Power of Attorney for Health Care?

A. Yes. You may provide, if you so choose, that if you are in a coma which your doctors have reasonably concluded is irreversible, that you desire that life-sustaining or prolonging treatments or procedures not be used. You may also provide, if you

More Questions and More Answers

so choose, that if you have an incurable or terminal condition or illness and no reasonable hope of long term recovery or survival, that you desire that life sustaining or prolonging treatments not be used.

Q. Can I exercise my right to prolong my life as long as possible in my Durable Power of Attorney for Health Care?

A. Yes. You may provide, if you so choose, that you desire that your life be prolonged to the greatest extent possible, without regard to your condition, the chances you have for recovery or long term survival or the costs of the procedures.

Q. What if I want to give the person I select to make my health care decisions some latitude on life sustaining procedures?

A. You may, if you so choose, provide that you do not desire treatment to be provided or continued if the burdens of the treatment outweigh the expected benefits and that the person you select to make your health care decisions is to consider the relief of suffering, the preservation or restoration of functioning and the quality as well as the extent of the possible extension of your life.

Q. Does my Durable Power of Attorney for Health Care have to be notarized or witnessed?

A. Your Durable Power of Attorney for Health Care must be either notarized or signed by two qualified witnesses who are known to you and were present when you signed or acknowledged your signature. The person you selected to be the one to make your health care decisions is disqualified to act as a witness or as the notary.

Q. When the Living Trust is finally dissolved, is there any probate necessary?

A. No. When all assets from the Living Trust have been distributed to your heirs, the Living Trust just ceases to exist.

Q. Are any of the legal fees for preparing an estate plan tax deductible?

A. If you have an A-B Trust or an A-B-C Trust, a portion of the legal fee attributable to tax planning is deductible as a miscellaneous itemized deduction on Form 1040 Schedule A. Only miscellaneous deductions above 2% of your adjusted gross income are allowed to reduce your taxable income. Make sure to request your

Chapter 10

More Questions and More Answers

attorney to allocate a portion of your
bill to tax planning if you establish
an A-B Trust or an A-B-C Trust.

Appendix A
Intestate Succession Rules

If a California resident dies without a will, his or her estate goes to the highest ranking class of survivors, as follows:

Community and Quasi-Community Property

• Surviving Spouse.
• If no surviving spouse, then to children or their descendants.
• If no surviving spouse or children or descendants of children, then to parents. If only one parent survives, all goes to the surviving parent, otherwise to parent's descendants if both are deceased.
• If no surviving spouse, children, parent or descendants of any of them, then to the nearest other surviving ancestors (grandparents, grand uncles and grand aunts, great grandparents, etc.), but not to their descendants.
• If no surviving spouse, children, parents, or descendants of children or par-ents, or ascendant relatives, then to nearest collateral relatives (aunts, uncles, cousins, etc.).
• If no living kin, then to the State of California.

Separate Property

• Surviving spouse and children or children's descendants. If no children or children's descendants, all to surviving spouse. If one child or his or her descendants, 1/2 to surviving spouse and 1/2 to child or his or her descendants. If two or more children or their descendants, 1/3 to surviving spouse and 2/3 to children or their descendants.
• If no surviving spouse, then to children or their descendants.
• If no surviving children or their descendants, then 1/2 to surviving spouse and 1/2 to parents and parent's descendants (except if only one parent sur-

Intestate Succession Rules

vives, he or she takes the entire share of the parents).

- If no surviving children or their descendants and no surviving parents or their descendants, then to surviving spouse.
- If no surviving spouse, no surviving children or their descendants, then to parents. If only one parent survives, all goes to the surviving parent, otherwise to parent's descendants if both are deceased.
- If no surviving spouse, children, parent or descendants of any of them, then to nearest other surviving ancestors (grandparents, grand uncles and grand aunts, great grandparents, etc.), but not to their descendants.
- If no surviving spouse, children, parents, or descendants of children or parents, or ascendant relatives, then to nearest collateral relatives (aunts, uncles, cousins, etc.).
- If no living kin, then to the State of California.

Property Attributable to a Predeceased Spouse (in cases where deceased was not survived by a spouse or children or their descendants and owned property received from a predeceased spouse, which had been either the predeceased spouse's separate property or community property, these special rules apply as to that property only).

- Children of predeceased spouse or their descendants.
- If no surviving children of the predeceased spouse or their descendants, then to parents of the predeceased spouse. If only one parent survives, all goes to the surviving parent, otherwise to parent's descendants if both are deceased.
- If no surviving children or parents or descendants if any of them of predeceased spouse, then to nearest surviving heir of the deceased.
- If no surviving children or parents or descendants of any of them of predeceased spouse and no surviving kin of the deceased, then to nearest surviving kin of predeceased spouse.
- If no surviving kin of either the deceased or the predeceased spouse, then to the State of California.

Appendix B
Affidavit to Exclude Small Estate from Probate

The undersigned declares:

1. I make this affidavit to induce ___ _____ to transfer to me the property described below under California Probate Code §§ 13100-13115.

2. _____(decedent) died at _____while a resident of the City of _____County of _____State of California, on or about_____,19____, leaving _____will.

3. At least 40 days have elapsed since the death of the decedent, as shown in a certified copy of the decedent's death certificate attached to this affidavit.

4. No proceeding is now being conducted or has been conducted in California for the administration of decedent's estate.

5. The gross value of the decedent's real and personal property in California, excluding the property described in California Probate Code § 13050, does not exceed $60,000 and includes the following: _____

_____

_____

9. The affiant requests that the described property be paid, delivered or transferred to the affiant.

10. I agree to hold _____free and harmless and indemnify _____ against all liability, claims, demands, losses, damages, costs and expenses whatsoever that _____ _____may incur because of said transfer, payment or delivery.

Appendix B

Affidavit to Exclude Small Estate from Probate

Dated: _____, 19____

Signature:_____

County of _____)
)
State of California _____)

    Subscribed and sworn to before me
        this _____day _____
        of _____, 19 ___.

_____

Notary Public
My commission expires on

_____

[Seal]

Appendix C

Probate Fee Chart

California Probate Code Section 901 sets forth the combined statutory fees for attorneys and executors based on the gross estate as follows:

	Gross Estate	Combined Statutory Fee
First	$ 15,000	8%
Next	85,000	6%
Next	900,000	4%
Next	9,000,000	2%
Next	15,000,000	1%
Over	25,000,000	Reasonable Compensation

Gross Estate	Combined Statutory Fee
$ 100,000	$ 6,300
200,000	10,300
300,000	14,300
400,000	18,300
500,000	22,300
600,000	26,300
700,000	30,300
800,000	34,300
900,000	38,300
1,000,000	42,300
1,100,000	44,300
1,200,000	46,300
1,300,000	48,300
1,400,000	50,300
1,500,000	52,300
1,600,000	54,300
1,700,000	56,300
1,800,000	58,300
1,900,000	60,300
2,000,000	62,300
3,000,000	82,300

Appendix C

Probate Fee Chart

Gross Estate	Combined Statutory Fee
4,000,000	102,300
5,000,000	122,300
6,000,000	142,300
7,000,000	162,300
8,000,000	182,300
9,000,000	202,300
10,000,000	222,300
15,000,000	272,300
20,000,000	322,300
25,000,000	372,300

Appendix D
Estate Tax Rate Chart

Effective Rates After Unified Credit

Taxable Amount Over	Taxable Amount Not Over	Tax on Amount in First Column	Effective Tax Rate on Excess Over Amount in First Column
$ 600,000	$ 750,000	-0-	37%
750,000	1,000,000	$55,500	39%
1,000,000	1,250,000	153,000	41%
1,250,000	1,500,000	255,000	43%
1,500,000	2,000,000	363,000	45%
2,000,000	2,500,000	588,000	49%
2,500,000	3,000,000	833,000	53%
3,000,000	—	1,098,000	55%

Appendix E

Comparison of A-B Trust with A-B-C Trust

The A-B-C Trust should be used only if your net estate is likely to exceed $1,200,000 at the date of the death of the first spouse to die <u>and</u> you wish to insure that the first spouse to die will control ultimate disposition of his or her one-half community property instead of just $600,000. There are no tax advantages available with an A-B-C Trust that you cannot obtain with an A-B Trust. Assume an estate of $1,600,000 on the death of the first spouse...

With an A-B Trust

<u>A</u>	<u>B</u>
$1,000,000	$600,000

With an A-B-C Trust

<u>A</u>	<u>B</u>	<u>C</u>
$ 800,000	$600,000	$200,000

The surviving spouse's interest goes in the A Trust and the decedent spouse's interest goes in the B and C Trusts. No more than $600,000 should ever be put in the B Trust or there will be an immediate estate tax.

The surviving spouse is entitled to all the income and principal of the A Trust and all of the income from the B and C Trusts. If the surviving spouse has consumed the A Trust or if it is impractical to use the principal of the A Trust (i.e., invested in a residence) then the survivor may use the principal of the B and C Trusts for the survivor's care, support and maintenance.

The advantage of an A-B-C Trust is that the surviving spouse may only give his or her one-half of the community property ($800,000 in our example) to a second spouse. With an A-B Trust, the surviving spouse controls all assets in excess of $600,000 ($1,000,000 in our example). Further, the creditors of the surviving

Appendix E

Comparison of A-B Trust with A-B-C Trust

spouse may not attach assets in the B and C Trusts.

The disadvantages of an A-B-C Trust are: (1) the surviving spouse must maintain three sets of records; and (2) the surviving spouse has less flexibility because he or she may not use the principal of either the B or C Trust unless he or she has exhausted the assets in the A Trust.

We normally recommend that you use the A-B-C Trust if you expect your net worth to exceed $1,200,000 on the death of the first spouse; and

(a) Either spouse has children of a former marriage; or

(b) Either spouse is concerned that his or her children may not inherit his or her one-half interest in the trust estate in excess of $600,000, on the death of the second spouse.

Appendix F

Single Person's Savings with Living Trust

In general, a single person's economic benefit in establishing a Living Trust instead of the ordinary will is limited to saving the costs of probate. A single person may also avoid conservatorship costs, of course, but since conservatorship costs do not occur in every case and are difficult to predict, they haven't been included in our chart. Following are the combined statutory probate fees that will be saved for gross estates of the sizes indicated:

Gross Estate	Combined Statutory Fee
$ 100,000	$6,300
200,000	10,300
300,000	14,300
400,000	18,300
500,000	22,300
600,000	26,300
700,000	30,300
800,000	34,300
900,000	38,300
1,000,000	42,300
1,100,000	44,300
1,200,000	46,300
1,300,000	48,300
1,400,000	50,300
1,500,000	52,300
1,600,000	54,300
1,700,000	56,300
1,800,000	58,300
1,900,000	60,300
2,000,000	62,300
3,000,000	82,300
4,000,000	102,300
5,000,000	122,300
6,000,000	142,300
7,000,000	162,300
8,000,000	182,300
9,000,000	202,300
10,000,000	222,300
15,000,000	272,300
20,000,000	322,300
25,000,000	372,300

Appendix G

Married Couple's Savings with Living Trust

The following table shows estimated savings for a husband and wife in terms of potential estate tax and probate costs using a Living Trust instead of an ordinary will. Because of the number of variables, it is not possible to exactly predict the savings available. We have assumed that on the death of the first spouse to die one-half of the estate will be probated and there will be no estate taxes. On the death of the second spouse to die, we assume that all of the estate will be probated and all of the estate will be subject to estate taxes, with no provision for any deductions for probate or other costs. It is also assumed that the amount of the taxable estate will be the same for both the first and the second death.

$100,000

Probate savings	$9,600
Estate tax savings	-0-
Total Savings	$9,600

$200,000

Probate savings	$16,600
Estate tax savings	-0-
Total Savings	$16,600

$300,000

Probate savings	$22,600
Estate tax savings	-0-
Total Savings	$22,600

$400,000

Probate savings	$28,600
Estate tax savings	-0-
Total Savings	$28,600

$500,000

Probate savings	$34,600
Estate tax savings	-0-
Total Savings	$34,600

$600,000

Probate savings	$40,600
Estate tax savings	-0-
Total Savings	$40,600

Appendix G

Married Couple's Savings with Living Trust

$700,000

Probate savings	$46,600
Estate tax savings	37,000
Total Savings	$83,600

$800,000

Probate savings	$ 52,600
Estate tax savings	75,000
Total Savings	$127,600

$900,000

Probate savings	$ 58,600
Estate tax savings	114,000
Total Savings	$172,600

$1,000,000

Probate savings	$ 64,600
Estate tax savings	153,000
Total Savings	$217,600

$1,100,000

Probate savings	$ 68,600
Estate tax savings	194,000
Total Savings	$262,600

$1,200,000

Probate savings	$ 72,600
Estate tax savings	235,000
Total Savings	$307,600

$1,300,000

Probate savings	$ 76,600
Estate tax savings	240,000
Total Savings	$316,600

$1,400,000

Probate savings	$ 80,600
Estate tax savings	245,000
Total Savings	$325,600

$1,500,000

Probate savings	$ 84,600
Estate tax savings	249,000
Total Savings	$333,600

$1,600,000

Probate savings	$ 88,600
Estate tax savings	255,000
Total Savings	$343,600

$1,700,000

Probate savings	$ 92,600
Estate tax savings	259,000
Total Savings	$351,600

$1,800,000

Probate savings	$ 96,600
Estate tax savings	263,000
Total Savings	$359,600

$1,900,000

Probate savings	$100,600
Estate tax savings	266,000
Total Savings	$366,600

$2,000,000

Probate savings	$104,600
Estate tax savings	268,000
Total Savings	$372,600

Married Couple's Savings with Living Trust

$2,500,000

Probate savings	$119,600
Estate tax savings	290,000
Total Savings	$409,600

$3,000,000

Probate savings	$134,600
Estate tax savings	314,000
Total Savings	$448,600

$3,500,000

Probate savings	$149,600
Estate tax savings	328,000
Total Savings	$477,600

$4,000,000

Probate savings	$164,600
Estate tax savings	330,000
Total Savings	$494,600

$4,500,000

Probate savings	$179,600
Estate tax savings	330,000
Total Savings	$509,600

$5,000,000

Probate savings	$194,600
Estate tax savings	330,000
Total Savings	$524,600

$6,000,000

Probate savings	$224,600
Estate tax savings	330,000
Total Savings	$554,600

$7,000,000

Probate savings	$254,600
Estate tax savings	330,000
Total Savings	$584,600

$8,000,000

Probate savings	$284,600
Estate tax savings	330,000
Total Savings	$614,600

$9,000,000

Probate savings	$314,600
Estate tax savings	330,000
Total Savings	$644,600

$10,000,000

Probate savings	$344,600
Estate tax savings	330,000
Total Savings	$674,600

For estates of more than $10,000,000 the estate tax benefit of the unified credit is phased out by adding an additional 5% tax on amounts up to $21,040,000 ($18,340,000 after December 31, 1992). Probate fees continue at 1% of the excess over $10,000,000 until the probate estate reaches $25,000,000. After $25,000,000, probate fees are based on "reasonable compensation."

Appendix H

Estate Planning Glossary

We have tried to keep the terminology used in this book as non-technical and understandable as possible. Many of the terms defined in this glossary have been used in the book, but many others have not. We're including the additional terms here because you may have heard or seen them used in other estate planning discussions.

Abatement. Reduction in the amount of bequest under a will because the estate is insufficient to pay all debts, probate costs and taxes.

Accumulation Trust. A trust that does not pay out all of its income.

Administrator. The person named by the court to represent the estate when there is no will or the will did not name an executor. Also sometimes called a personal representative.

Anatomical Gift. A gift of a portion of body at death.

Ancillary Probate. Probate undertaken in another state or country. Ancillary probates are necessary in each state or country in which you own real property. If the property were owned by a Living Trust the ancillary probates would not be necessary.

Annual Exclusion. The annual amount exempt from gift tax. The current amount exempt is $10,000 per donor per donee per year.

Annuity Trust. A trust that pays a fixed amount annually and then goes to a charity when the beneficiary dies.

Asset. Things a person owns, such as real property, stocks, bank accounts, etc.

Attestation. The statement at the end

of a will that is signed by the witnesses.

Basis. Generally, the basis is the original cost of an asset. The taxable gain on the sale of an asset is the net sales price less adjusted basis. Basis is adjusted by several factors, including costs of certain improvements to the property. Basis is also "stepped-up" on the death of the owner of the property to the value at the date of death. The amount of the step-up in basis depends on how title to the property was held by the deceased owner.

Beneficiary. The individual or other entity who receives the benefit of the transaction.

Bequest. A gift of personal property at death. A gift of real property at death is called a devise.

By Right of Representation. To a person's descendants by class. If you leave an asset to your issue by right of representation, a deceased child's portion will go to his or her children in equal shares. If you leave an asset to your children "per capita," a deceased child's portion will be equally divided among your surviving children. By right of representation is also sometimes called "per stirpes."

By-Pass Trust. Another name for the B Trust or the Decedent Spouse's Trust.

Codicil. An amendment to a will. The codicil is a separate document which modifies, adds to or revokes the provisions in the will, which must be signed with the same formalities as a will. A codicil may also be changed or revoked at any time.

Community Property. Property owned in common by husband and wife in a kind of marital partnership in which both husband and wife have a present vested, equal, undivided interest. Generally all earnings of both parties and all property acquired from those earnings during the marriage are community property. Community property is only recognized in eight states, including California.

Conservator. The individual appointed by the court to manage the affairs of an incapacitated adult.

Conservator of the Estate. The individual appointed by the court to manage the assets of an incapacitated adult.

Conservator of the Person. The individual appointed by the court to manage the personal care of an incapacitated adult.

Conservatorship. A court proceeding to appoint a manager (the Conservator) for the financial affairs and personal care of an adult who is mentally or physically unable to do so.

Corpus. The property owned by a trust is often referred to as the "trust corpus" or the "corpus of the trust." It is also sometimes called the "trust res."

Credit Shelter Trust. Another name for the B Trust or the By-Pass Trust.

Custodian. A person or entity appointed to deal with a minor's assets. Until the minor reaches majority (age 18) or becomes emancipated, the custodian manages the property and spends on the minor's behalf so much of the custodial property and income from the property as the custodian deems necessary for the support, maintenance, education and benefit of the minor.

Death Income Tax. The capital gains tax due on the sale of an asset that received a step-up in basis at the death of the previous owner or co-owner.

Decedent Spouse's Trust. Another name for the B Trust or the By-Pass Trust.

Deep Discount Bonds. Bonds issued by the federal government at a discount from face value that can be used at face value to pay estate taxes. Sometimes also called "flower bonds."

Descent. Property that passes at death.

Devise. Gift of real property at death. A gift of personal property at death is called a bequest.

Devisee. The person who receives real property under a will.

Discharge. The release of an executor or administrator after probate is over.

Disclaimer. The refusal to inherit an asset, allowing it to go to another person.

Domicile. A person's legal residence.

Donee. Person who receives a gift.

Donor. Person who makes a gift.

Durable General Power of Attorney. A general power of attorney that will continue to be valid after its maker becomes incapacitated or incompetent.

Durable Power of Attorney for Health Care. A special power of attorney that

Estate Planning Glossary

will continue to be valid after its maker becomes incapacitated or incompetent. It enables the maker to appoint another person to make health care decisions in the event he or she can no longer do so.

Estate Tax. A transfer tax imposed on the net value of the property left at death.

Executor. The person or other entity nominated in a will to take care of a deceased's property after his or her death. Executors are sometimes called personal representatives. A female executor is sometimes referred to as an "executrix," although most modern documents refer to both males and females as "executors."

Fee Simple. Complete ownership of real property.

Fiduciary. A person or other entity in a position of trust with regard to another. For example, executors, trustees, custodians and guardians are all fiduciaries. The law imposes a higher standard of care on one acting in a fiduciary capacity than one acting at arms-length.

Five-Plus-Five Power. The right to withdraw from a trust either 5% of its value or $5,000 each year, whichever is greater. Surviving spouses may be given the five-plus-five power with regard to

the B Trust after the death of the first spouse to die.

Flower Bonds. Another term for deep discount bonds.

Future Interest. A gift in which the recipient does not get the benefit, use or enjoyment until sometime in the future. The $10,000 annual gift tax exclusion is only for gifts of present interests and not for gifts of future interests.

Generation-Skipping Trust. A trust that skips giving the principal to the first generation. For example, a trust that pays all income to a child during his or her lifetime, with the principal payable to the child's children at the child's death.

Gift Tax. A tax imposed on the transfer of property by gift during the donor's lifetime. This is a federal tax. California does not have a separate gift tax.

Grantor. The person or other entity who makes a grant of property to another person. The grantor of a trust is also sometimes called a trustor or a settlor.

Grantor Trust. The name the IRS uses for the Living Trust.

Gross Estate Tax. The estate tax before the deduction of the unified credit.

Guardian of the Estate. The person who is appointed to manage the assets of a minor.

Guardian of the Person. The person who is appointed to raise a minor.

Heirs. Technically, those persons the government selects to receive assets when there is no will. Throughout this book, we have used the term "heirs" more generically to include anyone receiving assets on the death of another, whether by will, by Living Trust or by intestate succession.

Holographic Will. A will written entirely in a person's own handwriting that was dated and signed at the bottom. No witnesses are required under California law for a holographic will.

Income. Earnings, such as interest, dividends and rent. Income does not include capital gains, which are gains in the value of the property that have been realized.

Independent Administration of Estate. Powers given by the probate court to an executor or administrator to do more without prior court approval than would otherwise be allowed.

Inheritance Tax. A separate state tax in addition to the federal estate tax. In 1982 David E. Miller, one of the co-authors of this book, sponsored an initiative which was passed by the voters that abolished the California inheritance tax.

Inter Vivos Trust. A trust created to take effect during the lifetime of its maker. The Living Trust is a revocable inter vivos trust.

Intestate. A person who dies without a valid will.

Intestate Succession. The statutory rules on who receives the property of a person who dies without a valid will.

Inventory. The list of assets and values subject to probate proceedings.

Irrevocable Trust. A trust whose terms cannot be revoked or modified. However, under certain limited circumstances, a court can modify or even revoke an irrevocable trust. The Insurance Trust and the Children's Trust are both irrevocable trusts. Also, the B Trust and the C Trust become irrevocable trusts after the death of the first spouse.

Estate Planning Glossary

Issue. Generally, all natural and adopted descendants, whether legitimate or illegitimate, of unlimited generations.

Joint Tenancy. A form of joint property ownership where the survivor automatically becomes the owner of the property on the death of the co-owner, without probate. A will has no power to change the joint tenant's right of survivorship.

Joint Will. A single will signed by two or more people.

Lapsed Gift. An asset that fails to pass at death because the beneficiary is deceased.

Legacy. An asset that passes by a will. Both devises and bequests are legacies.

Letters Testamentary. The legal document giving the executor or administrator the authority to handle the decedent's assets. Sometimes just called "letters."

Life Estate. Right to use an asset for life only. The holder of a life estate cannot pass the asset at his or her death.

Life Insurance Trust. An irrevocable trust which is established for the purpose of excluding life insurance proceeds from the estate of the insured for estate tax purposes. Also called an Insurance Trust or an Irrevocable Life Insurance Trust.

Marital Deduction. The amount you may give to your spouse free of estate or gift taxes. This amount is currently unlimited.

Mutual Will. Separate wills signed by spouses with substantially identical provisions.

Net Estate Tax. The estate tax after the deduction of the unified credit.

Notice of Death. Legal notice that is published and mailed by the executor or administrator to creditors of the deceased.

Nuncupative Will. An oral will. At one time an oral will in a death-bed situation was valid for personal property, but not for real property, in California. Oral wills are no longer valid in California for any purpose.

Per Capita. All members of the class take equally. If a member of the class is deceased, the gift does not go to the deceased person's descendants (as it would if the gift were "per stirpes"). It goes instead to the other members of the class in equal shares.

Per Stirpes. Same as "by right of representation."

Personal Property. Generally, all property that is not real property. Movable property, such as cash, securities, furniture, automobiles, jewelry, etc.

Personal Representative. Another name for an executor or an administrator.

Pour Over Will. A will that transfers the decedent's assets that are subject to the will to a trust that was already in effect prior to the decedent's death. Pour Over Wills used with Living Trusts are intended as an insurance policy to make sure assets that were unintentionally left outside the Living Trust during lifetime are at least placed in the Living Trust after death.

Power of Appointment. Control of the disposition of another person's property subject to the power. A general power of appointment allows the person exercising the power to give the property to anyone, including the person who granted the power. A special power of appointment allows the person exercising the power to give the property only to certain specified individuals or groups. Property

subject to a general power of appointment is includable in the estate of the grantor of the power for estate tax purposes. Property subject to a special power of appointment is not includable in the estate of the grantor of the power for estate tax purposes. If the holder of the power can transfer the property to the grantor, the grantor's estate, the grantor's creditors or the grantor's estate's creditors, it is treated as a general power of appointment and is includable in the grantor's estate for estate tax purposes.

Pretermitted Heir. Certain relatives, such as spouse, children and sometimes grandchildren, who, if not mentioned at all in a will, will still get part of the decedent's assets.

Qualified Terminable Interest Property Trust. Another name for the Q-TIP Trust or the C Trust. Property in this trust is allowed to escape estate taxes on the death of the first spouse, and yet the decedent may control the disposition of the property after the death of the surviving spouse. The surviving spouse is entitled to all income from the property, payable at least annually.

Quasi-Community Property. All personal property and real property located in the State of California owned by Cali-

Estate Planning Glossary

fornia residents that was acquired while living outside of California which would have been community property had it been acquired while living in California.

Real Property. Land or things permanently affixed to the land and minerals under the land.

Remaindermen. The people who receive the assets of a trust when it terminates.

Res. The property owned by a trust is often referred to as the "trust res" or the "res of the trust." It is also sometimes called the "trust corpus."

Residuary. What is left after all specific gifts have been made. Also called the residue.

Reversions. Assets that go to another person because a condition was not met.

Revocable Trust. A trust that can be altered or revoked by the person who created the trust. The Living Trust is a revocable trust.

Rule Against Perpetuities. An ancient common law rule still in effect that says that all trusts must terminate within the lifetime of all those persons named in

the trust who are living when the trust takes effect plus twenty-one years.

Separate Property. Property acquired prior to marriage; property that was received by gift; property that was received by inheritance; the income from any of the foregoing property. If separate property is co-mingled with community property such that its separate character can no longer be accurately traced, it becomes community property.

Settlor. Another name for trustor or grantor. All three words mean the "maker" of the trust.

Specific Gift. A specific asset (for example, a diamond ring) left in a will.

State Death Tax Credit. The portion of the federal estate tax that will be forgiven if it goes instead to the state where the decedent died. California abolished its inheritance tax by a voter's initiative sponsored by David E. Miller, but continues to collect the maximum state death tax credit amount.

Surety Bond. The bond required for an executor or administrator unless the will waives it. The premiums are paid out of the estate.

Surviving Spouse's Trust. Another name for the A Trust.

Tenancy by the Entirety. A special joint tenancy for married couples. Not recognized in California.

Tenancy in Common. A form of joint ownership of property. There is no right of survivorship with your tenant in common. Each tenant in common has the right to dispose of his or her interest by means of a will or by placing the interest in a Living Trust.

Testamentary Trust. A trust that only comes into existence at the death of the maker of the trust.

Testate. One who dies with a valid will.

Testator. The maker of a will. "Testatrix" is sometimes used for a female testator, but most modern documents use "testator" for both males and females.

Testamentary Capacity. The legal ability to make a will.

Trust. A fiduciary relationship in which a person (called either a trustor, grantor or settlor) transfers legal title of property to a fiduciary (trustee), who manages the property for the benefit of someone (beneficiary).

Trust Estate. The assets in the trust. Sometimes also referred to as the trust corpus or the trust res.

Trustee. The person or other entity given legal title to the property by the trustor to hold and manage it for the benefit of the beneficiary in accordance with the trustor's written instructions.

Trustor. The person or other entity that establishes a trust. Also called a grantor or a settlor in some cases.

Unified Credit. An estate and gift tax credit of up to $192,800 which permits the transfer of up to $600,000 free of estate and gift taxes (or up to $1,200,000 for a married couple with an A-B Trust or an A-B-C Trust).

Widow's Election. A provision in a will that gives the widow or widower a choice of either (1) allowing the decedent's portion of the community property to pass under the decedent's will rather than the surviving spouse's will when the surviving spouse dies; or (2) being disinherited from the decedent's spouse's portion of the community property.

187

Appendix I

Summary of the Complete Estate Plan

Following is a summary of important matters that we recommend you include in your Complete Estate Plan:

<u>Living Trust</u>, with the following clauses:

- Identification of the original trustors, trustees and beneficiaries.
- Identification of successor trustees.
- Identification of successor beneficiaries.
- Identification of property held in the Living Trust and, if married, identification of all such property as community property or as separate property of husband or wife.
- Provisions making the Living Trust either an A Trust, an A-B Trust or an A-B-C Trust.
- Delay of distribution until successor beneficiaries reach specified ages, such as 1/3 of principal at age 25, 1/3 at age 30 and 1/3 at age 35 with net income payable monthly.
- Identification of trustee's powers, such as the power to borrow money, the power to collateralize assets, the power to buy and sell assets, etc.
- Provisions allowing a co-trustee or a successor trustee to take over administration of the Living Trust in case of incompetency.
- A Creditors Clause, which allows a successor trustee to probate any asset to take advantage of the shorter statute of limitations if an estate goes through probate.
- A Catastrophic Illness Clause, which allows married trustors to divide their community property into separate property in the event one of them has a catastrophic illness.
- A No Contest Clause, which disinherits anyone contesting the Living Trust.
- A provision allowing for compensation of successor trustees.

Appendix I

Summary of the Complete Estate Plan

- Provisions making the Living Trust a Qualified Domestic Trust if a spouse is not a U.S. citizen.
- A provision naming the Living Trust; e.g., THE 1985 HILL FAMILY TRUST.
- A provision for the situs (legal location) of the Living Trust; e.g., the situs of the Living Trust of California residents would normally be California and California laws would govern the Living Trust.

Pour Over Will, which puts any assets you failed to put in the Living Trust during your lifetime in the Living Trust at your death. This document also selects the guardian for your minor or incapacitated children.

Assignment of Personal Property, which puts assets that are not registered such as clothing, household goods, etc. into the Living Trust.

Letter of Instruction Regarding Personal Property, which is the instruction to your co-trustee or successor trustee on how to distribute your personal effects upon your death.

Community Property Declaration, which changes your joint tenancy property to community property if you are married.

Durable General Power of Attorney, which allows someone you select to place your assets into the Living Trust should you become incompetent before you can do so yourself.

Durable Power of Attorney for Health Care, which allows someone you select to make health care decisions for you should you become unable to do so. This document also allows you to exercise your right to die if you so choose.

Directive to Physicians, which is your own direction to your physicians exercising your right to die. This document is sometimes call a Living Will.

Nomination of Conservator, which gives someone the legal authority to care for your person, as distinguished from your assets, if you become incompetent. Your Living Trust is designed to avoid conservatorship of your assets, but if you are unable to care for yourself physically you need a conservator of your person.

Schedule of Assets, which is simply a list of your assets which are in your Living Trust.

Summary of the Complete Estate Plan

<u>Location Schedule</u>, which is an instruction to your co-trustee or successor trustee on where to find your assets and important papers.

<u>Funeral and Burial Instructions and Anatomical Gift</u>, which provide your instructions that need to be followed shortly after your death.

<u>Miscellaneous Trusts</u>, such as the Insurance Trust, Children's Trust, etc., which may be applicable in certain specialized situations. These are separate trusts from your Living Trust.

Appendix J

Instructions for Funding Your Living Trust

After you sign your Living Trust, you must still transfer your assets to the Living Trust before it will become fully effective for you. If you fail to transfer an asset into the Living Trust, you risk having it subjected to conservatorship proceedings during your lifetime and probate proceedings after your death.

Listing assets in the back of your Living Trust document in Schedules A, B and C is important because it's a convenient list of the assets you intend to be in the Living Trust (for both unmarried and married trustors) and because it separates your property into community property, separate property of the husband and separate property of the wife (for married couples only). However, listing assets in the Schedules <u>does not transfer the assets into the Living Trust</u>. This must be done separately for each asset as described below.

Drive carefully until you transfer all your assets into your Living Trust!

<u>Real Property</u>: To change the title of real property to your Living Trust you must record a new grant deed in the county in which the property is located. For California property, you are also required to file a Preliminary Change of Ownership Report, indicating that the transfer is to a Living Trust so that the transfer is exempt from reassessment under Proposition 13. Most counties will charge a recording fee of around $9.00.

We recommend that you have your attorney prepare the grant deed and Preliminary Change of Ownership Report. This is one of the few times you should need an attorney in funding your Living Trust. Once the documents are prepared, you can file them with the county recorder's office yourself. If you have real estate in other states or countries, you should contact an attorney in that jurisdiction to complete the transfer.

If you refinance your real estate after

Instructions for Funding Your Living Trust

it is in your Living Trust, many financing agencies will require that the real estate be removed from the Living Trust. Ask them to prepare a grant deed changing title from the Living Trust to your name as an individual and then borrow the money. After the transaction is closed, ask the title company to prepare a new grant deed putting the real estate back into your Living Trust.

Promissory Notes Receivable: If someone owes you money and signed a promissory note payable to you, you will want to assign that promissory note to your Living Trust. You can do that by endorsing the front or reverse side of the promissory note as follows:

"I (we) assign my (our) interest in the within promissory note to [your name(s)], Trustee(s), U.D.T., dated (the date you signed your Living Trust)"

Deeds of Trust: If you have loaned money or sold property to someone and receive a promissory note which is secured by a deed of trust on real estate, then you should assign the deed of trust to your Living Trust as well as the promissory note.

We recommend that you have your attorney prepare the assignment of the deed of trust. This is one of the few times you will need an attorney in funding your Living Trust. Once the document is prepared, you can record it with the country recorder's office yourself. Most counties will charge a recording fee of around $9.00.

Partnership Interests. If you have a limited partnership interest, you should write a letter to the general partner requesting an assignment of your interest to the Living Trust, in the following form:

"I (we) have established a Living Trust. Please change my (our) ownership interest to [your name(s)], Trustee(s), U.D.T., dated (the date you signed your Living Trust)"

If you are a general partner, you should review the partnership agreement, if any, to determine if it requires the written consent of the other partners before you can assign your interest to your Living Trust. If it does require such consent, then send a letter to the other general partners, asking for their written consent to the transfer, in the following form:

"I (we) wish to transfer my (our) partnership interest to my (our) Living Trust. If you consent to this transfer, please sign a copy of this letter and return it to me (us)."

After receiving the consent, prepare an assignment in the following form:

"Assignment

I (we) assign my (our) interest in that Partnership Agreement, dated (date of the agreement), between (names of the parties), to [your name(s)], Trustee(s), U.D.T., dated (date you signed your Living Trust).

(Date of assignment) [Your signature(s)]
Dated   [Your name(s)]"

Closely Held Corporations: If you own stock in a closely held corporation, a new stock certificate should be issued for the same number of shares to "[your name(s)], Trustee(s), U.D.T., dated (date you signed your Living Trust)"

You must also cancel the previously issued certificate. Fill out the assignment section on the back of the old certificate, sign it and mark the face of the certificate CANCELLED.

Sole Proprietorships: You should assign your interest in the business to your Living Trust by preparing an assignment in the following form:

"Assignment

I (we) assign my (our) interest in that business known as (name and address of business) to [your name(s)], Trustee(s), U.D.T., dated (date you signed your Living Trust).

(Date of assignment) [Your signature(s)]
Dated   [Your name(s)]"

Stocks and Bonds: It is necessary for you to change the title of your securities from you as an individual to you as trustee of your Living Trust. To transfer and re-register securities you hold in your own name, you will need a form of assignment which is usually called a "stock power". You can obtain this form from your stock broker or from the company that issued you your stock. The stock power form usually requires that your signature be guaranteed either by your securities firm or a commercial bank. After completing the form you will return it to your broker or the issuing company requesting them to re-register your securities as "[your name(s)], Trustee(s), U.D.T., dated (date you signed your Living Trust)." You will be required to surrender your old stock certificates before new ones are issued. You will usually also have to provide a

Instructions for Funding Your Living Trust

copy of your Living Trust.

Instead of actually having certificates for your stocks and bonds, you may just have a brokerage account with a securities broker. If so, your stocks and bonds are held in "street name" which means the certificates are actually issued in the name of the securities broker or its nominee. In that case, you have to change title to the account you have with the securities broker rather than on the individual certificates. You can do so by writing a letter to your broker in the following form:

"I (we) have established a Living Trust. Please change the ownership of account number(s) (list all account numbers you have with the broker) to [your name(s)], Trustee(s), U.D.T., dated (date you signed your Living Trust)."

Savings Accounts, Certificates of Deposit, Money Market Accounts and Treasury Bills: These accounts should all be retitled "[your name(s)], Trustee(s), U.D.T., dated (date you signed your Living Trust)."

The bank officer will usually ask to see a copy of your Living Trust. In filling out the signature card to open the account, you would normally indicate that either trustee (if you are married) may sign on the account.

Prior to changing title of these accounts to your Living Trust, you should determine if the transfer will result in the loss of any interest. If the particular account cannot be transferred without the loss of interest, you may decide to wait until maturity of the account to make the transfer.

E.E. Bonds: You must obtain Treasury Form PD 1851 (call the Federal Reserve Bank at (415) 974-2060). Fill out the form and take it to a bank or savings and loan for a signature guarantee. Make a copy of the form and your Bonds and take the original and your E.E. Bonds directly to the Federal Reserve Bank of San Francisco at 101 Market Street (they close at 3:00 p.m.). They will review the forms and the E.E. Bonds and give you a signed receipt. In 4 to 8 weeks the Federal Reserve will send the re-registered E.E. Bonds back to you.

Personal Property: We recommend that you assign your personal property, such as clothing, jewelry, furniture, etc. to your Living Trust by using an Assignment of Personal Property form that your attorney should provide you at the time you sign your Living Trust.

Gold, Silver and Rare Coins: If there is a certificate evidencing the ownership of these assets, then you must have the title on the certificate changed to reflect the new ownership to "[your name(s)], Trustee(s), U.D.T., dated (date you signed your Living Trust)."

If there is no certificate, then you must prepare an assignment similar to the following form:

"Assignment

I (we) assign all of my (our) gold, silver and rare coins located at (address of location) to [your name(s)], Trustee(s), U.D.T., dated (date you signed your Living Trust).

(Date of Assignment)   [Signature(s)]
Dated   [Your name(s)]"

Copyrights: You must assign your copyrights to your Living Trust by following the form set forth in the paragraph regarding gold, silver and rare coins. You must also notify the U.S. Copyright Office.

Municipal Bonds: You must contact the issuing municipality or your broker and have the title of the bonds changed to your Living Trust.

Checking Accounts: We recommend that most married couples keep a small personal checking account in joint ten-

ancy rather than in the Living Trust for convenience. Unmarried people and married couples who maintain large balances in their checking accounts may want to transfer their accounts to their Living Trust. If so, follow the instructions in the paragraph on savings accounts.

Motor Vehicles and Motor Homes: Most married couples should hold these assets as joint tenants until the death of the first spouse. The transfer to the Living Trust should take place after the death of the first spouse. Unmarried people can transfer motor vehicles to their Living Trust. You must go to the Department of Motor Vehicles. You will have to provide them with a copy of your Living Trust. They will provide you with the proper forms. Among them should be an Endorsement of Ownership Certificate. This certificate must contain the name of the Living Trust and the trustee. As an example:

1985 Hill Living Trust
Jill Hill, Trustee
100 Nobb Hill Street
San Francisco, CA 94102

Signature: 1985 Hill Living Trust
          By: Jill Hill
          Trustee

Instructions for Funding Your Living Trust

<u>Retirement Plan Benefits</u>: Since these proceeds automatically avoid probate, we generally recommend that your spouse be the primary beneficiary and if your children are adults, that they be the secondary beneficiaries. If your children are minors, or if you are delaying distribution of assets to them until they reach certain ages, then we recommend that the Living Trust should be secondary beneficiary. If you are an unmarried person, your Living Trust would normally be named the primary beneficiary.

Do not change the <u>ownership</u> of your retirement plans to your Living Trust.

<u>Life Insurance and Annuities</u>: Unless you need a Life Insurance Trust, your Living Trust should be the beneficiary of your life insurance and annuities. You may obtain designation of beneficiary forms from the life insurance company insuring your life. The beneficiary would be listed as "The (<u>your last name</u>) Living Trust, dated (<u>the date you signed your Living Trust</u>)." Example: "The Hill Living Trust, dated March 1, 1985."

<u>Safe Deposit Boxes</u>: These boxes must be in the names of individuals. You cannot have your Living Trust listed as the owner of a safe deposit box. You can, however, transfer the <u>contents</u> of the safe deposit box to the Living Trust. You might consider naming your co-trustee or successor trustee on the account for the safe deposit box.

Trust I.D. Numbers

Your stockbroker, banker or insurance agent may ask for the federal tax identification number of your Living Trust. Tell them that Living Trusts are no longer required to have federal tax identification numbers. They should use your social security number.

Proving Existence of Your Trust

When you transfer the title of your various assets into your Living Trust, the companies involved may ask you to provide proof that your Living Trust exists and is valid and that you, as trustee, have the power to transfer assets into the Living Trust.

You may make as many copies of the Living Trust document as you wish. Usually, you can satisfy this request by supplying the companies with copies of the first page, the last numbered page containing your signature and the pages containing the powers of the trustee. This way you can prove the validity of the Living Trust and your powers as trustee without disclosing the distributive provisions of your Living Trust.

Some companies may insist on seeing your entire Living Trust document. In this case you either have to comply with their request or take your business elsewhere. There should never be the need for any of these companies to see your schedule of assets. They should not be sent even if you are sending copies of the rest of your Living Trust document.

Change of Assets

Once you've funded your Living Trust, remember to acquire new assets in the name of the Living Trust. If you sell or acquire an asset, remember to amend your schedules. You can amend your schedules without the assistance of an attorney in most cases; however, you should not attempt to amend any other portion of your Living Trust without consulting an attorney first.

Recording Documents

It is necessary to record deeds, deeds of trust and assignments of deeds of trust with the county recorder's office in the county where each piece of real estate is located. It is not necessary or desirable to record your Living Trust.

Appendix K

Checklist of Things to be Done at Death

- Check to see if decedent left funeral and burial instructions.
- Check to see if decedent wanted to make an anatomical gift.
- Call mortuary and make funeral and burial arrangements.
- Make a list of immediate family, friends and employer. Notify each by phone.
- If the deceased lived alone:
  (a) Make sure residence is secure and notify landlord;
  (b) Remove valuables and important documents to a safe place;
  (c) Contact utility companies to discontinue services; and
  (d) Arrange for forwarding of mail.
- Collect information for obituary and call newspaper. Include age, place of birth, cause of death, occupation, college degrees, memberships held, military service, outstanding work, survivors' names and date and place of funeral service. This is optional. If you publish the date of the funeral service, make sure someone is at the family residence during the funeral service because burglars often read obituaries.
- Prepare list of persons to be notified by letter or printed notice.
- Contact the attorney who prepared the Living Trust and obtain instructions.
- Obtain at least five certified copies of the death certificate from the mortuary.
- Assemble important papers, such as the Living Trust, bank books, stock certificates, real estate deeds, insurance policies, etc.
- Distribute personal effects in accordance with the Letter of Instruction Regarding Personal Property.
- Arrange to have any appreciated assets valued. Real estate should be appraised.
- Each insurance company should be provided with a statement of claim and a death certificate.

Appendix K

Checklist of Things to be Done at Death

- Contact the nearest Social Security Office for benefits. Benefits vary according to the number and age of children and age of the surviving spouse.
- If the deceased was a veteran, application should be made for Veterans Administration benefits. Benefits differ depending on whether or not the death was service-connected. In either case, maximum reimbursement for burial expenses is $250.
- Contact the deceased's employer and, if applicable, union or professional group. A formal letter requesting information about life and health insurance policies could provide additional data on coverage.
- Current installment loan, service contracts and credit card bills should be gathered together, since some may be covered by credit life insurance, which pays off all or part of the outstanding balance on the death of a customer. Similarly, there should be a check to see if the deceased had a mortgage insurance policy, which repays the outstanding mortgage upon the death of the policy holder.
- If credit cards were in joint names, removed deceased's name from the credit cards. If credit cards were in deceased's name alone, cancel the credit cards.
- Locate evidence of indebtedness due the estate by careful search. Examine the deceased's checkbooks, tax returns and other financial records for this purpose.
- Notify automobile insurance company for immediate cancellation and refund of unused portion of policy.
- Change any casualty insurance policies to eliminate the deceased as a named beneficiary.
- Make a list of any claims against the estate. Contact attorney if any of the claims are disputed.
- Contact Department of Motor Vehicles and banks to terminte joint tenancies.
- Change title of deceased's assets to co-trustee, successor trustee or successor beneficiary as applicable. An attorney should be used to transfer title to real estate, but most other transfers can be done without legal assistance.
- Contact your accountant. If you have an A-B Trust or an A-B-C Trust, assets have to be allocated to the appropriate trusts and a tax I.D. number will have to be obtained for the B and the C Trusts.
- If the estate of the deceased exceeds $600,000, have your accountant file a 706 federal estate tax return. Dates are vital. Penalties and interest are charged on late returns. Start on this as soon as possible.
- State and federal income tax returns

Checklist of Things to be Done at Death

still have to be filed and taxes paid. Income taxes are not excused by death. A surviving spouse may still file a joint return for the year of death of the deceased spouse.

Appendix L

Federal Tax Returns

Included on the following pages are:

- Federal Estate Tax Return—Form 706

- Federal Gift Tax Return—Form 709

- Federal Fiduciary Income Tax Return—Form 1041

Form **706**	United States Estate (and Generation-Skipping Transfer) Tax Return	OMB No. 1545-0015

Form **706**
(Rev. October 1988)
Department of the Treasury
Internal Revenue Service

United States Estate (and Generation-Skipping Transfer) Tax Return

Estate of a citizen or resident of the United States (see separate instructions). To be filed for decedents dying after October 22, 1986, and before January 1, 1990.
For Paperwork Reduction Act Notice, see page 1 of the Instructions.

OMB No. 1545-0015
Expires 8-30-91

Part 1.—Decedent and Executor

1a Decedent's first name and middle initial (and maiden name, if any)	**1b** Decedent's last name	**2** Decedent's social security no.
3a Domicile at time of death	**3b** Year domicile established	**4** Date of birth	**5** Date of death

6a Name of executor (see instructions)	**6b** Executor's address (number and street including apartment number or rural route; city, town, or post office; state; and ZIP code)
6c Executor's social security number (see instructions)	

7a Name and location of court where will was probated or estate administered	**7b** Case number

8 If decedent died testate, check here ▶ ☐ and attach a certified copy of the will. **9** If Form 4768 is attached, check here ▶ ☐

10 If Schedule R-1 is attached, check here ▶ ☐ *See page 2 for representative's authorization.*

Part 2.—Tax Computation

1	Total gross estate (from Part 5, Recapitulation, page 3, item 10).	**1**	
2	Total allowable deductions (from Part 5, Recapitulation, page 3, item 25)	**2**	
3	Taxable estate (subtract line 2 from line 1)	**3**	
4	Adjusted taxable gifts (total taxable gifts (within the meaning of section 2503) made by the decedent after December 31, 1976, other than gifts that are includible in decedent's gross estate (section 2001(b))).	**4**	
5	Add lines 3 and 4	**5**	
6	Tentative tax on the amount on line 5 from Table A in the instructions	**6**	

Note: *If decedent died before January 1, 1988, skip lines 7a-c and enter the amount from line 6 on line 8.*

7a	If line 5 exceeds $10,000,000, enter the lesser of line 5 or $21,040,000. If line 5 is $10,000,000 or less, skip lines 7a and 7b and enter zero on line 7c	**7a**	
b	Subtract $10,000,000 from line 7a	**7b**	
c	Enter 5% (.05) of line 7b	**7c**	
8	Total tentative tax (add lines 6 and 7c)	**8**	
9	Total gift tax payable with respect to gifts made by the decedent after December 31, 1976. Include gift taxes paid by the decedent's spouse for split gifts (section 2513) only if the decedent was the donor of these gifts and they are includible in the decedent's gross estate (see instructions)	**9**	
10	Gross estate tax (subtract line 9 from line 8)	**10**	
11	Unified credit against estate tax from Table B in the instructions.	**11**	
12	Adjustment to unified credit. (This adjustment may not exceed $6,000. See instructions.)	**12**	
13	Allowable unified credit (subtract line 12 from line 11)	**13**	
14	Subtract line 13 from line 10 (but do not enter less than zero)	**14**	
15	Credit for state death taxes. Do not enter more than line 14. Compute credit by using amount on line 3 less $60,000. See Table C in the instructions and **attach credit evidence** (see instructions)	**15**	
16	Subtract line 15 from line 14	**16**	
17	Credit for Federal gift taxes on pre-1977 gifts (section 2012)(attach computation)	**17**	
18	Credit for foreign death taxes (from Schedule(s) P). (Attach Form(s) 706CE)	**18**	
19	Credit for tax on prior transfers (from Schedule Q)	**19**	
20	Total (add lines 17, 18, and 19)	**20**	
21	Net estate tax (subtract line 20 from line 16)	**21**	
22	Generation-skipping transfer taxes (from Schedule R, Part 2, line 12)	**22**	
23	Section 4980A increased estate tax (attach Schedule S (Form 706)) (see instructions)	**23**	
24	Total transfer taxes (add lines 21, 22, and 23)	**24**	
25	Prior payments. Explain in an attached statement	**25**	
26	United States Treasury bonds redeemed in payment of estate tax	**26**	
27	Total (add lines 25 and 26)	**27**	
28	Balance due (subtract line 27 from line 24)	**28**	

Under penalties of perjury, I declare that I have examined this return, including accompanying schedules and statements, and to the best of my knowledge and belief, it is true, correct, and complete. Declaration of preparer other than the executor is based on all information of which preparer has any knowledge.

Signature(s) of executor(s) _____ Date _____

Signature of preparer other than executor _____ Address (and ZIP code) _____ Date _____

Estate of:

Part 3.—Elections by the Executor

Please check the "Yes" or "No" box for each question.

		Yes	No
1	Do you elect alternate valuation?		
2	Do you elect special use valuation? . . . . If "Yes," you must complete and attach Schedule A–1		
3	Do you elect to pay the taxes in installments as described in section 6166? . . . . If "Yes," you must attach the additional information described in the instructions.		
4	Do you elect to postpone the part of the taxes attributable to a reversionary or remainder interest as described in section 6163?		
5	Do you elect to have part or all of the estate tax liability assumed by an Employee Stock Ownership Plan (ESOP) as described in section 2210? If "Yes," enter the amount of tax assumed by the ESOP here ▶$ _____ and attach the supplemental statements described in the instructions.		

Part 4.—General Information Note: *Please attach the necessary supplemental documents.* **You must attach the death certificate.**

Authorization to receive confidential tax information under Regulations section 601.502(c)(3)(ii), to act as the estate's representative before the Internal Revenue Service, and to make written or oral presentations on behalf of the estate if return prepared by an attorney, accountant, or enrolled agent for the executor:

Name of representative (print or type)	State	Address (number and street, city, state, and ZIP code)

I declare that I am the attorney/accountant/enrolled agent (strike out the words that do not apply) for the executor and prepared this return for the executor. I am not under suspension or disbarment from practice before the Internal Revenue Service and am qualified to practice in the state shown above.

Signature	CAF Number	Date	Telephone Number

1 Death certificate number and issuing authority (attach a copy of the death certificate to this return).

2 Decedent's business or occupation. If retired, check here ▶ ☐ and state decedent's former business or occupation.

3 Marital status of the decedent at time of death:

☐ Married

☐ Widow or widower—Name, SSN and date of death of deceased spouse ▶ _____

_____

☐ Single
☐ Legally separated
☐ Divorced—Date divorce decree became final ▶

4a Surviving spouse's name	4b Social security number	4c Amount received (see instructions)

5 Individuals (other than the surviving spouse), trusts, or other estates who receive benefits from the estate (do not include charitable beneficiaries shown in Schedule O) (see instructions). For Privacy Act Notice (applicable to individual beneficiaries only), see the Instructions for Form 1040.

Name of individual, trust or estate receiving $5,000 or more	Identifying number	Relationship to decedent	Amount (see instructions)

All unascertainable beneficiaries and those who receive less than $5,000 . . . . ▶	
Total	

(Continued on next page)

Part 4.—General Information *(continued)*

	Please check the "Yes" or "No" box for each question.	Yes	No
6	Does the gross estate contain any section 2044 property (see instructions)?		
7a	Have Federal gift tax returns ever been filed?		
	If "Yes," please attach copies of the returns, if available, and furnish the following information:		

7b Period(s) covered	7c Internal Revenue office(s) where filed

If you answer "Yes" to any of questions 8–16, you must attach additional information as described in the instructions.

		Yes	No
8a	Was there any insurance on the decedent's life that is not included on the return as part of the gross estate?		
b	Did the decedent own any insurance on the life of another that is not included in the gross estate?		
9	Did the decedent at the time of death own any property as a joint tenant with right of survivorship in which (1) one or more of the other joint tenants was someone other than the decedent's spouse, and (2) less than the full value of the property is included on the return as part of the gross estate? If "Yes," you must complete and attach Schedule E		
10	Did the decedent, at the time of death, own any interest in a partnership or unincorporated business or any stock in an inactive or closely held corporation?		
11a	Did the decedent make any transfer described in section 2035, 2036, 2037 or 2038 (see the instructions for Schedule G)? If "Yes," you must complete and attach Schedule G		
b	If "Yes," was it a valuation freeze subject to section 2036(c)?		
12	Were there in existence at the time of the decedent's death:		
a	Any trusts created by the decedent during his or her lifetime?		
b	Any trusts not created by the decedent under which the decedent possessed any power, beneficial interest, or trusteeship?		
13	Did the decedent ever possess, exercise, or release any general power of appointment? If "Yes," you must complete and attach Schedule H.		
14	Was the marital deduction computed under the transitional rule of Public Law 97-34, section 403(e)(3) (Economic Recovery Tax Act of 1981)? If "Yes," attach a separate computation of the marital deduction, enter the amount on item 18 of the Recapitulation, and note on item 18 "computation attached."		
15	Was the decedent, immediately before death, receiving an annuity described in the "General" paragraph of the instructions for Schedule I? If "Yes," you must complete and attach Schedule I.		
16	Did the decedent have a total "excess retirement accumulation" (as defined in section 4980A(d)) in qualified employer plan(s) and individual retirement plan(s)? If "Yes," you must attach Schedule S (Form 706) (see instructions)		

Part 5.—Recapitulation

Item number	Gross estate	Alternate value	Value at date of death
1	Schedule A—Real Estate		
2	Schedule B—Stocks and Bonds		
3	Schedule C—Mortgages, Notes, and Cash		
4	Schedule D—Insurance on the Decedent's Life (attach Form(s) 712)		
5	Schedule E—Jointly Owned Property (attach Form(s) 712 for life insurance)		
6	Schedule F—Other Miscellaneous Property (attach Form(s) 712 for life insurance) . .		
7	Schedule G—Transfers During Decedent's Life (attach Form(s) 712 for life insurance)		
8	Schedule H—Powers of Appointment		
9	Schedule I—Annuities		
10	Total gross estate (add items 1 through 9). Enter here and on line 1 of the Tax Computation.		

Item number	Deductions	Amount
11	Schedule J—Funeral Expenses and Expenses Incurred in Administering Property Subject to Claims	
12	Schedule K—Debts of the Decedent	
13	Schedule K—Mortgages and Liens	
14	Total of items 11 through 13	
15	Allowable amount of deductions from item 14 (see the instructions for item 15 of the Recapitulation)	
16	Schedule L—Net Losses During Administration	
17	Schedule L—Expenses Incurred in Administering Property Not Subject to Claims	
18	Schedule M—Bequests, etc., to Surviving Spouse	
19	Schedule O—Charitable, Public, and Similar Gifts and Bequests	
20	Total of items 15 through 19—If you did not complete Schedule N, skip lines 21-24 and enter the line 20 amount on line 25 .	
21	Intermediate taxable estate (subtract item 20 from item 10)	
22	Maximum ESOP deduction (from Table D in the Instructions)	
23	Enter the amount from Schedule N, line 8.	
24	Allowable ESOP deduction—enter the lesser of item 22 or 23	
25	Total allowable deductions (add items 20 and 24). Enter here and on line 2 of the Tax Computation	

Form **709**
(Rev. December 1989)
Department of the Treasury
Internal Revenue Service

United States Gift (and Generation-Skipping Transfer) Tax Return

(Section 6019 of the Internal Revenue Code) (For gifts made after December 31, 1988, and before January 1, 1990)

Calendar year 19 _ _ _ _ _

► **See separate instructions. For Privacy Act Notice, see the Instructions for Form 1040.**

OMB No. 1545-0020
Expires 11-30-92

Part 1.—General Information

1 Donor's first name and middle initial	2 Donor's last name	3 Social security number

4 Address (number and street)	5 Domicile

6 City, state, and ZIP code	7 Citizenship

	Yes	No
8 If the donor died during the year, check here ► ☐ and enter date of death _ _ _ _ _ _ _ _ _ _ _ _ _ _ _ _ _ , 19 _ _ _ _ .		
9 If you received an extension of time to file this Form 709, check here ►☐ and attach the Form 4868, 2688, 2350, or extension letter.		
10 If you (the donor) filed a previous Form 709 (or 709-A), has your address changed since the last Form 709 (or 709-A) was filed?		
11 Gifts by husband or wife to third parties.—Do you consent to have the gifts (including generation-skipping transfers) made by you and by your spouse to third parties during the calendar year considered as made one-half by each of you? (See instructions.) (If the answer is "Yes," the following information must be furnished and your spouse is to sign the consent shown below. If the answer is "No," skip lines 12–17 and go to Schedule A.).		

12 Name of consenting spouse	13 SSN		

14 Were you married to one another during the entire calendar year? (See instructions.)		
15 If the answer to 14 is "No," check whether ☐ married ☐ divorced or ☐ widowed, and give date (see instructions) ►		
16 Will a gift tax return for this calendar year be filed by your spouse?		

17 **Consent of Spouse**—I consent to have the gifts (and generation-skipping transfers) made by me and by my spouse to third parties during the calendar year considered as made one-half by each of us. We are both aware of the joint and several liability for tax created by the execution of this consent.

Consenting spouse's signature ►　　　　　　　　　　　　　　　　　　　　　Date ►

Part 2.—Tax Computation

1	Enter the amount from Schedule A, Part 3, line 15	1
2	Enter the amount from Schedule B, line 3	2
3	Total taxable gifts (add lines 1 and 2)	3
4	Tax computed on amount on line 3 (see Table for Computing Tax in separate instructions)	4
5a	Enter the lesser of line 3 or $21,040,000	**5a**
b	Subtract $10,000,000 from line 5a (do not enter less than zero)	**5b**
c	Enter 5% (.05) of line 5b	5c
6	Total tentative tax on the amount on line 3 (add lines 4 and 5c)	6
7	Tax computed on amount on line 2 (see Table for Computing Tax in separate instructions)	7
8a	Enter the lesser of line 2 or $21,040,000	**8a**
b	Subtract $10,000,000 from line 8a (do not enter less than zero)	**8b**
c	Enter 5% (.05) of line 8b	8c
9	Total tentative tax on the amount on line 2 (add lines 7 and 8c)	9
10	Balance (subtract line 9 from line 6)	10
11	Maximum unified credit (nonresident aliens, see instructions)	11	192,800	00
12	Enter the unified credit against tax allowable for all prior periods (from Sch. B, line 1, col. C)	12
13	Balance (subtract line 12 from line 11)	13
14	Enter 20% (.20) of the amount allowed as a specific exemption for gifts made after September 8, 1976, and before January 1, 1977 (see instructions)	14
15	Balance (subtract line 14 from line 13)	15
16	Unified credit (enter the smaller of line 10 or line 15).	16
17	Credit for foreign gift taxes (see instructions)	17
18	Total credits (add lines 16 and 17).	18
19	Balance (subtract line 18 from line 10) (do not enter less than zero)	19
20	Generation-skipping transfer taxes (from Schedule C, Part 4, col. H, total)	20
21	Total tax (add lines 19 and 20)	21
22	Gift and generation-skipping transfer taxes prepaid with extension of time to file . . .	22
23	If line 22 is less than line 21, enter BALANCE DUE (see instructions)	23
24	If line 22 is greater than line 21, enter AMOUNT TO BE REFUNDED	24

Please attach check or money order here

Under penalties of perjury, I declare that I have examined this return, including any accompanying schedules and statements, and to the best of my knowledge and belief it is true, correct, and complete. Declaration of preparer (other than donor) is based on all information of which preparer has any knowledge.

Donor's signature ►　　　　　　　　　　　　　　　　　　　　　Date ►

Preparer's signature (other than donor) ►　　　　　　　　　　　　　　Date ►

Preparer's address (other than donor) ►

For Paperwork Reduction Act Notice, see page 1 of the separate instructions for this form.

Form **709** (Rev. 12-89)

SCHEDULE A   Computation of Taxable Gifts

Part 1.—Gifts Subject Only to Gift Tax. *Gifts less political organization, medical, and educational exclusions—see instructions*

A Item number	B Donee's name, relationship to donor (if any), and address and description of gift. If the gift was made by means of a trust, enter trust's identifying number below and attach a copy of the trust instrument. If the gift was securities, enter the CUSIP number(s), if available.	C Donor's adjusted basis of gift	D Date of gift	E Value at date of gift
1				

Part 2.—Gifts Which are Direct Skips and are Subject to Both Gift Tax and Generation-Skipping Transfer Tax. You must list the gifts in chronological order. *Gifts less political organization, medical, and educational exclusions—see instructions*

A Item number	B Donee's name, relationship to donor (if any), and address and description of gift. If the gift was made by means of a trust, enter trust's identifying number below and attach a copy of the trust instrument. If the gift was securities, enter the CUSIP number(s), if available.	C Donor's adjusted basis of gift	D Date of gift	E Value at date of gift
1				

Part 3.—Gift Tax Reconciliation

1	Total value of gifts of donor (add column E of Parts 1 and 2)	1	
2	One-half of items _____ attributable to spouse (see instructions)	2	
3	Balance (subtract line 2 from line 1)	3	
4	Gifts of spouse to be included (from Schedule A, Part 3, line 2 of spouse's return—see instructions) .	4	

If any of the gifts included on this line are also subject to the generation-skipping transfer tax, check here ▶ ☐ and enter those gifts also on Schedule C, Part 1.

5	Total gifts (add lines 3 and 4)	5	
6	Total annual exclusions for gifts listed on Schedule A (including line 4, above) (see instructions) . .	6	
7	Total included amount of gifts (subtract line 6 from line 5)	7	

Deductions (see instructions)

8	Gifts of interests to spouse for which a marital deduction will be claimed, based on items _____ of Schedule A . . .	8		
9	Exclusions attributable to gifts on line 8	9		
10	Marital deduction—subtract line 9 from line 8	10		
11	Charitable deduction, based on items _____ to _____ less exclusions	11		
12	Total deductions—add lines 10 and 11		12	
13	Subtract line 12 from line 7		13	
14	Generation-skipping transfer taxes payable with this Form 709 (from Schedule C, Part 4, col. H, Total)		14	
15	Taxable gifts (add lines 13 and 14). Enter here and on line 1 of the Tax Computation on page 1 . .		15	

(If more space is needed, attach additional sheets of same size.)

SCHEDULE A   Computation of Taxable Gifts (continued)

16 Terminable Interest (QTIP) Marital Deduction. (See instructions.)

☐ ◄ Check here if you elected, under the rules of section 2523(f), to include gifts of qualified terminable interest property on line 8, on page 2. Enter the item numbers (from Schedule A) of the gifts for which you made this election ► -

SCHEDULE B   Gifts From Prior Periods

Did you (the donor) file gift tax returns for prior periods? (If "Yes," see instructions for completing Schedule B below.) . . . . ☐ Yes   ☐ No

A Calendar year or calendar quarter (see instructions)	B Internal Revenue office where prior return was filed	C Amount of unified credit against gift tax for periods after December 31, 1976	D Amount of specific exemption for prior periods ending before January 1, 1977	E Amount of taxable gifts

1 Totals for prior periods (without adjustment for reduced specific exemption) **1**

2 Amount, if any, by which total specific exemption, line 1, column D, is more than $30,000 . . . . . **2**

3 Total amount of taxable gifts for prior periods (add amount, column E, line 1, and amount, if any, on line 2)
(Enter here and on line 2 of the Tax Computation on page 1.) **3**

SCHEDULE C   Computation of Generation-Skipping Transfer Tax

Note: *Inter vivos direct skips which are completely excluded by the grandchild exclusion and/or the GST exemption must still be fully reported (including value and exclusions and exemptions claimed) on Schedule C.*

Part 1.—Generation-Skipping Transfers

A Item No. (from Schedule A, Part 2, col. A)	B Value (from Schedule A, Part 2, col. E)	C Split Gifts (enter ½ of col. B) (see instructions)	D Subtract col. C from col. B	E Annual Exclusion Claimed	F Subtract col. E from col. D	G Grandchild Exclusion Claimed	H Net Transfer (subtract col. G from col. F)
1							
2							
3							
4							
5							
6							
7							
8							

	Split gifts from spouse's Form 709 (enter item number)	Value included from spouse's Form 709			
If you elected gift splitting and your spouse was required to file a separate Form 709 (see the instructions for "Split Gifts"), you must enter all of the gifts shown on Schedule A, Part 2, of your spouse's Form 709 here. In column C, enter the item number of each gift in the order it appears in column A of your spouse's Schedule A, Part 2. We have preprinted the prefix "S-" to distinguish your spouse's item numbers from your own when you complete column A of Schedule C, Part 4. In column D, for each gift, enter the amount reported in column C, Schedule C, Part 1, of your spouse's Form 709.	S- S- S- S- S- S- S- S- S-				
	Total grandchild exclusions claimed on this return. Must equal total of column D, Schedule C, Part 2				▨▨▨

(If more space is needed, attach additional sheets of same size.)

SCHEDULE C   Computation of Generation-Skipping Transfer Tax (continued)

Part 2.—Grandchild Exclusion Reconciliation

Name of Grandchild	A Maximum Allowable Exclusion	B Total of Exclusions Claimed on Previous Returns	C Exclusion Available for This Return (subtract col. B from col. A)	D Exclusion Claimed on this Return	E Exclusion Available for Future Returns (subtract col. D from col. C)
	$2,000,000				
	$2,000,000				
	$2,000,000				
	$2,000,000				
	$2,000,000				
	$2,000,000				
	$2,000,000				
	$2,000,000				

Total grandchild exclusions claimed on this return. Must equal total of column G, Part 1

Part 3.—GST Exemption Reconciliation (Code section 2631) and Section 2652(a)(3) Election

Check box ▶ ☐ if you are making a section 2652(a)(3) (special QTIP) election (see instructions)

Enter the item numbers (from Schedule A) of the gifts for which you are making this election ▶ _____

1	Maximum allowable exemption	**1**	$1,000,000
2	Total exemption used for periods before filing this return	**2**	
3	Exemption available for this return (subtract line 2 from line 1)	**3**	
4	Exemption claimed on this return (from Part 4, col. C total, below)	**4**	
5	Exemption allocated to transfers not shown on Part 4, below. You must attach a Notice of Allocation. (See instructions.)	**5**	
6	Add lines 4 and 5	**6**	
7	Exemption available for future transfers (subtract line 6 from line 3)	**7**	

Part 4.—Tax Computation

A Item No. (from Schedule C, Part 1)	B Net transfer (from Schedule C, Part 1, col. H)	C GST Exemption Allocated	D Divide col. C by col. B	E Inclusion Ratio (subtract col. D from 1.000)	F Maximum Gift Tax Rate	G Applicable Rate (multiply col. E by col. F)	H Generation-Skipping Transfer Tax (multiply col. B by col. G)
1					55% (.55)		
2					55% (.55)		
3					55% (.55)		
4					55% (.55)		
5					55% (.55)		
6					55% (.55)		
7					55% (.55)		
8					55% (.55)		
					55% (.55)		
					55% (.55)		
					55% (.55)		
					55% (.55)		
					55% (.55)		
					55% (.55)		
					55% (.55)		

Total exemption claimed. Enter here and on line 4, Part 3, above. May not exceed line 3, Part 3, above . . . . . .

Total generation-skipping transfer tax. Enter here, on line 14 of Schedule A, Part 3, and on line 20 of the Tax Computation on page 1 . . . .

(If more space is needed, attach additional sheets of same size.)

☆U.S. Government Printing Office: 1989-261-151/00034

Form **1041**

Department of the Treasury—Internal Revenue Service

U.S. Fiduciary Income Tax Return

1989

IRS Use Only

For the calendar year 1989 or fiscal year beginning _____ , 1989, and ending _____ , 19___   OMB No. 1545-0092

Check applicable boxes:

- ☐ Decedent's estate
- ☐ Simple trust
- ☐ Complex trust
- ☐ Grantor type trust
- ☐ Bankruptcy estate
- ☐ Family estate trust
- ☐ Pooled income fund
- ☐ Initial return
- ☐ Amended return
- ☐ Final return

Name of estate or trust (grantor type trust, see instructions)

Name and title of fiduciary

Address of fiduciary (number and street or P.O. Box)

City, state, and ZIP code

Number of Schedules K-1 attached (see instructions) . . . ▶

Employer identification number

Date entity created

Nonexempt charitable and split-interest trusts, check applicable boxes (see instructions):

- ☐ Described in section 4947(a)(1)
- ☐ Not a private foundation
- ☐ Described in section 4947(a)(2)

Income

1	Dividends	1
2	Interest income	2
3	Income (or losses) from partnerships, other estates, or other trusts (see instructions)	3
4	Net rental and royalty income (or loss) (attach Schedule E (Form 1040))	4
5	Net business and farm income (or loss) (attach Schedules C and F (Form 1040))	5
6	Capital gain (or loss) (attach Schedule D (Form 1041))	6
7	Ordinary gain (or loss) (attach Form 4797)	7
8	Other income (state nature of income) _____	8
9	**Total** income (add lines 1 through 8) . . . ▶	9

Deductions

10	Interest .	10	
11	Taxes .	11	
12	Fiduciary fees .	12	
13	Charitable deduction (from Schedule A, line 6)	13	
14	Attorney, accountant, and return preparer fees	14	
15a	Other deductions NOT subject to the 2% floor (attach schedule) .	15a	
b	Allowable miscellaneous itemized deductions subject to the 2% floor .	15b	
c	Add lines 15a and 15b	15c	
16	**Total** (add lines 10 through 15c) .		16
17	Adjusted total income (or loss) (subtract line 16 from line 9). Enter here and on Schedule B, line 1 . ▶		17
18	Income distribution deduction (from Schedule B, line 17) (see instructions) (attach Schedules K-1 (Form 1041))		18
19	Estate tax deduction (including certain generation-skipping transfer taxes) (attach computation) . .		19
20	Exemption		20
21	**Total** deductions (add lines 18 through 20) . . . ▶		21

Tax and Payments

22	Taxable income of fiduciary (subtract line 21 from line 17)	22
23	**Total** tax (from Schedule G, line 7) . . . ▶	23
24a	Payments: 1989 estimated tax payments and amount applied from 1988 return .	24a
b	Treated as credited to beneficiaries .	24b
c	Subtract line 24b from line 24a	24c
d	Tax paid with extension of time to file: ☐ Form 2758 ☐ Form 8736 ☐ Form 8800 . .	24d
e	Federal income tax withheld	24e
	Credits: **f** Form 2439 _____ ; **g** Form 4136 _____ ; **h** Other _____ ; Total ▶	24i
25	**Total** payments (add lines 24c through 24e, and 24i) . . . ▶	25
26	If line 23 is larger than line 25, enter **TAX DUE** . .	26
27	If line 25 is larger than line 23, enter **OVERPAYMENT** . .	27
28	Amount of line 27 to be: **a Credited to 1990 estimated tax** ▶ _____ ; **b Refunded** . ▶	28
29	**Penalty** for underpayment of estimated tax (see instructions) . . .	29

Please attach check or money order here

Please Sign Here

Under penalties of perjury, I declare that I have examined this return, including accompanying schedules and statements, and to the best of my knowledge and belief, it is true, correct, and complete. Declaration of preparer (other than fiduciary) is based on all information of which preparer has any knowledge.

▶ _____   _____   ▶ _____

Signature of fiduciary or officer representing fiduciary   Date   EIN of fiduciary (see instructions)

Paid Preparer's Use Only

Preparer's signature ▶	Date	Check if self-employed ▶ ☐	Preparer's social security no.
Firm's name (or yours if self-employed) and address ▶		E.I. No. ▶	
		ZIP code ▶	

For Paperwork Reduction Act Notice, see page 1 of the separate Instructions.

Form **1041** (1989)

Schedule A	**Charitable Deduction—Do not complete for a simple trust or a pooled income fund.**		

(Write the name and address of each charitable organization to whom your contributions total $3,000 or more on an attached sheet.)

1	Amounts paid or permanently set aside for charitable purposes from current year's gross income . . .	1	
2	Tax-exempt interest allocable to charitable distribution (see instructions)	2	
3	Subtract line 2 from line 1	3	
4	Enter the net short-term capital gain and the net long-term capital gain of the current tax year allocable to corpus paid or permanently set aside for charitable purposes (see instructions)	4	
5	Amounts paid or permanently set aside for charitable purposes from gross income of a prior year (see instructions)	5	
6	Total (add lines 3 through 5). Enter here and on page 1, line 13	6	

Schedule B	**Income Distribution Deduction (see instructions)**		

1	Adjusted total income (from page 1, line 17) (see instructions)	1	
2	Adjusted tax-exempt interest (see instructions)	2	
3	Net gain shown on Schedule D (Form 1041), line 17, column (a). (If net loss, enter zero.) . . .	3	
4	Enter amount from Schedule A, line 4	4	
5	Long-term capital gain included on Schedule A, line 1	5	
6	Short-term capital gain included on Schedule A, line 1	6	
7	If the amount on page 1, line 6, is a capital loss, enter here as a positive figure	7	
8	If the amount on page 1, line 6, is a capital gain, enter here as a negative figure	8	
9	Distributable net income (combine lines 1 through 8)	9	
10	Amount of income for the tax year determined under the governing instrument (accounting income) **10**		
11	Amount of income required to be distributed currently (see instructions)	11	
12	Other amounts paid, credited, or otherwise required to be distributed (see instructions)	12	
13	Total distributions (add lines 11 and 12). (If greater than line 10, see instructions.)	13	
14	Enter the total amount of tax-exempt income included on line 13	14	
15	Tentative income distribution deduction (subtract line 14 from line 13)	15	
16	Tentative income distribution deduction (subtract line 2 from line 9)	16	
17	Income distribution deduction. Enter the smaller of line 15 or line 16 here and on page 1, line 18 . . .	17	

Schedule G	**Tax Computation (see instructions)**		

1	Tax: **a** Tax rate schedule .... ; **b** Other taxes .... ; . . . . Total ▶		1c	
2a	Foreign tax credit (attach Form 1116)	2a		
b	Credit for fuel produced from a nonconventional source.	2b		
c	General business credit. Check if from: ☐ Form 3800 or ☐ Form (specify) ▶	2c		
d	Credit for prior year minimum tax (attach Form 8801)	2d		
3	**Total** credits (add lines 2a through 2d) . . . . ▶		3	
4	Subtract line 3 from line 1c.		4	
5	Recapture taxes. Check if from: ☐ Form 4255 ☐ Form 8611		5	
6	Alternative minimum tax (attach Form 8656)		6	
7	**Total** tax (add lines 4 through 6). Enter here and on page 1, line 23 . . . . ▶		7	

Other Information (see instructions) | **Yes** | **No**

1   If the fiduciary's name or address has changed, enter the old information ▶ --
    ----

2   Did the estate or trust receive tax-exempt income? (If "Yes," attach a computation of the allocation of expenses.) . . .
    Enter the amount of tax-exempt interest income and exempt-interest dividends ▶ $ ------------------

3   Did the estate or trust have any passive activity losses? (If "Yes," enter these losses on **Form 8582**, Passive Activity Loss Limitations, to figure the allowable loss.) . . . .

4   Did the estate or trust receive all or any part of the earnings (salary, wages, and other compensation) of any individual by reason of a contract assignment or similar arrangement? . . . .

5   At any time during the tax year, did the estate or trust have an interest in or a signature or other authority over a financial account in a foreign country (such as a bank account, securities account, or other financial account)? (See the instructions for exceptions and filing requirements for Form TD F 90-22.1.) . . . .
    If "Yes," enter the name of the foreign country ▶ --

6   Was the estate or trust the grantor of, or transferor to, a foreign trust which existed during the current tax year, whether or not the estate or trust has any beneficial interest in it? (If "Yes," you may have to file Form 3520, 3520-A, or 926.)

7   Check this box if this entity has filed or is required to file **Form 8264**, Application for Registration of a Tax Shelter . ▶ ☐

8   Check this box if this entity is a complex trust making the section 663(b) election . . . . ▶ ☐

9   Check this box to make a section 643(e)(3) election (attach Schedule D (Form 1041)) . . . . ▶ ☐

10 Check this box if the decedent's estate has been open for more than 2 years . . . . ▶ ☐

11 Check this box if the trust is a participant in a Common Trust Fund that was required to adopt a calendar year . . ▶ ☐